The Capital Drain: Why Uncertainty - Not Hurricanes - Breaks Insurance Markets

October 2024
Don D. Brown
DeFuniak Springs, FL 32435
www.dondbrown.live

Copyright Page

Published by Rebell Books
Atlanta, GA
ISBN: 978-1-967567-74-4

For permission requests, please contact:
Don D. Brown
don@dondbrown.com

Library of Congress Cataloging-in-Publication Data:
[Placeholder for Cataloging Information, if applicable]

Cover design by Don D. Brown
Printed in the United States of America
First Edition: 2025

“There is treasure to be desired and oil in the dwelling of the wise; but a foolish man spendeth it up.”
— Proverbs 21:20 (KJV)

“Store up during the years of plenty, so there will be food in the land during the years of famine.”
— Genesis 41 (KJV, paraphrased)

TABLE OF CONTENTS

Preface

What if the real storm isn't in the Gulf—it's in the rulebook? I wrote the original white paper that became this book after watching a familiar pattern: a bad season hits, capital flinches, premiums spike, and we tell ourselves the wind did it. But that's only half true. The other half is harder to admit. When statutes wobble, when courts broaden promises that were never priced, when timelines and penalties are written for blue-sky Tuesdays instead of gray-sky months, the market hears a siren it cannot ignore. Hurricanes break roofs; **uncertainty** breaks markets.

I learned long ago that the single most useful idea in economics comes down to a line: **risk can be priced; uncertainty cannot**. Risk has odds—even ugly odds. Uncertainty doesn't. If you honor that line, capital behaves. If you blur it, capital bolts. Over the years, I have sat across kitchen tables with homeowners trying to understand a renewal and across conference tables with reinsurers trying to understand a jurisdiction. Both households and balance sheets want the same thing: **known odds**. Give them that, and they will plan, invest, and rebuild. Deny them that, and they will leave.

This book is my attempt to make that line visible and practical for Florida and for any catastrophe-exposed place that wants a durable insurance market. We start with history—Hammurabi's schedules and Knight's distinction between risk and uncertainty—then move to psychology (Ellsberg's jellybeans), finance (how committees actually price wind), and policy (the habits that move a market left toward risk or right toward uncertainty). Along the way, I use metaphors to keep us honest. If you hear about poker with and without cards, ducks quacking in a different language, or a symphony that suddenly shifts to jazz, it's not for effect; it's because those images translate committee memos and statutory edits into something you can feel.[1, 2]

A word about tone. This book carries urgency because the costs of getting this wrong land on families who did nothing wrong. But I am also optimistic. We cannot stop hurricanes, but we can stop compounding them with man-made ambiguity. The playbook is not a mystery: write changes **prospectively**, draft **narrowly and plainly**, design claims for **catastrophe reality**, make **mitigation** the cheapest habit in the state, and keep a lifeboat (the residual market) that rows back to shore on a set schedule. Do those boring things, and Florida will earn the trust of balance sheets from London to Zurich. Don't do them, and we will keep waking up to the same renewal drama with new headlines and the same bill.

This began as a white paper. It grew into a short book because stakeholders kept asking for something they could hand to a colleague—or a legislator—that explains not only *what* to do but *why* it works. I have tried to write it so a homeowner, a city clerk, an agent, and an ILS manager can read the same pages and see their part in the machine. Where opinion shows, it is rooted in experience: years as an agent, years in public office, years arguing that **market discipline is consumer protection**. Predictability is not a gift to companies; it is justice for households who plan in good faith.

Two final notes. First, you will see a simple graphic—**Figure 2.1: The Risk–Uncertainty Spectrum**—repeated as a breadcrumb in several chapters. It's not decoration; it's the map. Ask of every reform, every contract clause, every claims protocol: *Does this move us left toward risk or right toward uncertainty?* Second, you'll see humor here and there. Policy is heavy work; a little levity keeps us from turning prudence into scolding. But the stakes are not a joke. When rules surprise, premiums become a quiet tax on prudence.

If we do this right, the next time a storm season tests us, roofs will still fail, but the market won't. Capital will show up priced to **peril**, not to **process**. And when Maria calls her agent a month after landfall, that call will be short. Not painless—never painless—but short. That is the measure of success I care about: how quickly life returns to normal after the world has leaned hard against your house.

— Don Brown

DeFuniak Springs, Florida

A Note on How to Read This Book

You can read straight through, but the book also works in parts.

1. **Chapter 1–3** build the intellectual backbone: history, Knight's line, Ellsberg's jellybeans, and why capital hates moving goalposts.
2. **Chapter 4–6** put Florida under the microscope—how storms, statutes, and spreads interact, and what investors actually see.
3. **Chapter 7–8** are the posture and the plan: Joseph's storehouses as pre-event discipline, and what a resilient Florida looks and feels like.

If you're a policymaker, focus on **Chapter 5–8** and the playbook sections. If you're in finance, **Chapter 3, 5, 6** will feel like home. If you're a homeowner, **Chapter 4, 7, 8** plus the mitigation pieces will save you money and grief. Throughout, watch for small **Spectrum Check** callouts—quick reminders to ask whether a choice moves the market left (priceable risk) or right (uncertainty).

We'll get to the **Appendix** later with a one-page "Calibrating the Spectrum" guide and a homeowner mitigation checklist. For now, keep Figure 2.1 in view. It's the north star.

A Note on Scope

While Florida's property insurance crisis provides the primary case study, the patterns identified here appear across markets globally. Whether you're concerned about healthcare in Arizona, solar energy in Spain, or flood insurance in the UK, the fundamental dynamics remain consistent: uncertainty drives capital away, and capital flight harms the very people policies aim to protect.

The choice of how deeply to engage is yours. Read it as a cautionary tale, use it as a reference manual, or apply it as a toolkit for reform. However you approach it, the message remains the same: in markets, as in life, it's not the storms we can see coming that destroy us, but the ground that shifts beneath our feet without warning.

Acknowledgments

A book like this stands on other people's shoulders. I owe thanks to the agents and adjusters who, during long hurricane seasons, took my calls after midnight and told me what was happening on real streets, not in sanitized memos. To the underwriters, brokers, reinsurers, and ILS managers who—sometimes grudgingly—walked me through their models and their misgivings. Your candor shaped these pages more than you know.

To public servants who still believe that predictability is a virtue: thank you for the unglamorous labor of hearings, drafting, and enforcement. You are the quiet reason programs place, premiums stabilize, and roofs go back on without drama. To consumer advocates who forced me to explain, not just assert, that market discipline is a form of mercy: you made the arguments sharper—and fairer.

To friends who offered early reads of the white paper that became this manuscript: you circled my jargon and underlined my optimism in equal measure. To the editors who tightened the prose and cut where I would not: you made a better book. Any errors that remain are mine alone.

Most of all, to the families who keep Florida running—teachers, small business owners, retirees on fixed incomes—who pay premiums in quiet faith that promises will be kept when the wind blows: you are the point of all this. If these pages help lower the quiet tax of uncertainty you've been paying, they will have done their job.

Finally, and personally, to my wife, Diane, for patience through late drafts and early mornings, and to our family for tolerating more talk of jellybeans, poker tables, ducks, and roof decks than anyone should have to endure. The support you've shown is the storehouse I draw from in lean seasons.

Introduction: Why Capital Flees

"May those that love us – love us.
And for those that don't, may God turn their heart.
And for those whose hearts He cannot turn, may He turn their ankle,
So that we will know them by their limping."

That old blessing always brings a smile. It reminds us that sometimes life offers only imperfect solutions—if we can't win people over, at least we can spot them limping toward us. Insurance markets, believe it or not, often operate the same way. When confidence falters, when rules shift unexpectedly, investors don't linger to argue. They limp—or rather, they run—for the exits.

Risk vs. Uncertainty: A Crucial Distinction

Economist Frank H. Knight once drew a line between two concepts that look similar but behave very differently: **risk** and **uncertainty**. Risk can be measured. A hurricane striking Florida in any given year has a probability we can model. We may not know *when*, but we can calculate the odds. That's risk.

Uncertainty, on the other hand, is the angry bear rowing your boat backward

—unpredictable, chaotic, and outside any actuarial table. Insurers and reinsurers can price risk; they cannot stomach uncertainty. And when uncertainty grows, capital flees. That is the heart of the capital drain.

A Florida Homeowner's Dilemma

Consider Maria, a middle-class homeowner in Miami. She budgets carefully, saves diligently, and pays her insurance premium every year. She understands the risk of hurricanes—she's lived through them before. What she doesn't understand is why her premium doubles overnight or why her insurer suddenly leaves the state.

For Maria, the storm outside isn't as frightening as the storm inside the marketplace. Risk she can live with; uncertainty she cannot plan for. And neither can the insurers who decide whether to keep her covered.

Why This Book?

This book is about that distinction—between risk that can be calculated and uncertainty that drives capital away. It's about how Florida, and by extension America's coastal states, have often blurred that line through short-term political tinkering. And it's about how we can learn from both history and principle—from Hammurabi's Babylon to Joseph's Egypt—to rebuild an insurance market that is not only fair but resilient.

The chapters that follow will explore:

1. The long tradition of risk-sharing that makes insurance indispensable.
2. Why Knight's insights on risk and uncertainty still matter.
3. How Florida became the world's laboratory for catastrophe and policy failure.
4. Why global capital treats hurricanes as manageable risk but views political meddling as unacceptable uncertainty.
5. And finally, how timeless wisdom—the Joseph Principle of saving in times of plenty—offers a path forward.

This book is a call to policymakers, industry leaders, and homeowners alike: if we do not address uncertainty, we will continue to suffer a capital drain that leaves us all more vulnerable when the next storm comes.

Chapter 1 – The Long Road of Risk: From Hammurabi to Hurricanes

A Story Written in Stone

If you were a merchant in Babylon nearly 4,000 years ago, your greatest fear wasn't high premiums—it was losing everything in one storm or raid. The Code of Hammurabi, carved into stone around 1750 B.C., contained a clause that changed commerce forever: if a merchant borrowed money to finance a shipment, he could pay an extra fee to cancel the loan if thieves or natural disaster struck. In essence, the lender shared the risk of loss.

This wasn't charity. It was practicality. Without such a mechanism, merchants would never have dared to send ships down dangerous rivers or caravans through lawless deserts. Insurance, in its most primitive form, was born: a way to spread the financial shock of loss so that trade could continue. The principle is the same today: risk pooling enables economic activity. No bank would finance a Florida subdivision, no investor would buy reinsurance bonds, if all the risk rested on the unlucky few. Risk-sharing works. [3]

Ancient Innovations

The Babylonians were not alone. In ancient China during the Zhou dynasty (1046–256 B.C.), merchants deliberately split their cargo among multiple boats. If one sank, the voyage wasn't a total loss. In Greece and Rome, traders used "bottomry" and "respondentia" contracts in which ship owners took loans secured by their vessels and cargo—if the ship went down, the loan was forgiven. And then there were the Roman collegia, guild-like societies that pooled resources to bury members and support widows and orphans.

The common thread? **Mutual protection.** These systems weren't profit-driven; they were resilience-driven. The idea was simple: if we all chip in, no single disaster destroys any one of us. That communal instinct laid the groundwork for the modern industry—and it also foreshadows a recurring theme in this book: markets function best when the rules for sharing losses are clear, consistent, and honored.

From Guild Halls to Fire Brigades

Fast forward to medieval Europe. As commerce expanded, so did risk. Fires, shipwrecks, and theft threatened livelihoods. To survive, guilds pooled funds to support members in times of loss. These guilds were early insurers, blending fraternity with finance.

By the 14th century, standalone insurance policies emerged in trading cities like Genoa and Florence. These were no longer just mutual promises—they were enforceable contracts, and risk itself had become a tradable commodity. Underwriters began to quantify hazards, to stipulate terms, to price the possibility of loss. Insurance was professionalizing.

Then came catastrophe on a metropolitan scale. In 1666, the **Great Fire of London** destroyed more than 13,000 houses and nearly bankrupted the city. In the ashes, Nicholas Barbon founded one of the first fire insurance companies, which not only insured property but also created fire brigades to mitigate risk. Suddenly, insurance wasn't only about paying for losses after the fact—it was about **reducing losses before they occurred**. Prevention entered the business model. [4]

Two decades later, Lloyd's of London coalesced out of a coffeehouse where shipowners, merchants, and financiers met to underwrite voyages. They shared and syndicated risks, standardized marine policies, and, through reputation and contract, built trust at global scale. What began as parchment contracts among seafarers became the foundation of modern insurance markets.

From Fate to Formula

For centuries, risk was seen as fate—the will of the gods, the turn of fortune's wheel. Beginning in the 17th century, human beings learned to measure it. **Probability theory** gave us a way to quantify uncertainty. **Edmund Halley's** mortality tables turned life expectancy into numbers on a page. **Actuarial science** transformed risk from mystery into mathematics.

By the 19th and 20th centuries, insurers could calculate everything from fire risk in dense tenements to crop failures across the plains. In the 21st century, insurers use big data, artificial intelligence, lidar, and satellite imagery to price risks from cyber intrusion to coastal flood. The arc of history is unmistakable: risk has moved from **fate** to **formula**. That shift is why banks can lend, investors can plan, and communities can rebuild after disaster. Insurance is the silent infrastructure that keeps promises payable.

But there is a boundary to what can be measured. On one side lies **risk**—measurable, modelable, priceable. On the other lies **uncertainty**—the domain of the unknown. Crossing that boundary is where markets wobble. (In Chapter 2, we will meet Frank H. Knight, who drew that line with enduring clarity.)

The American Story of Insurance

Insurance crossed the Atlantic with colonists. Benjamin Franklin helped found the **Philadelphia Contributionship for the Insurance of Houses from Loss by Fire** in 1752—the first successful mutual insurance company in the colonies. Franklin's company did more than sell policies; it inspected houses for fire hazards and refused coverage for dangerous construction. Risk-based pricing—and loss prevention—were thus enshrined in the American tradition.

As the young nation industrialized, insurance followed risk. Marine and fire insurers supported the rise of port cities; factory mutuals improved safety standards; life insurance expanded rapidly after the Civil War as families sought protection against breadwinner loss. By the early 20th century, automobile liability, workers' compensation, and group health transformed not just commerce but daily life. Every expansion followed the same pattern: risk-sharing enabled progress. Railroads could not have expanded, mortgages could not have proliferated, and hospitals could not have been built without insurance standing behind the promise that catastrophe would not destroy balance sheets.

America also innovated in **reinsurance**—insurance for insurers. By slicing, layering, and ceding portions of exposure to other carriers and global reinsurers, companies could write more policies without concentrating too much risk. Later, **insurance-linked securities** (ILS) and **catastrophe bonds** allowed capital markets to invest in catastrophe risk directly. These instruments matter in Florida because they are the bridge between local hazards and global capital.[5]

Economic Implications of Uncertainty (A One-Page Primer)

When uncertainty rises, capital does the math and backs away. New money slows; existing money demands wider spreads or higher attachment points; some capacity simply does not roll. With less risk capital available, primary carriers face higher costs and tighter terms, and those pressures migrate—first to reinsurance quotes, then to homeowner renewals. Over time, exits and consolidations concentrate the market, reducing competition and narrowing consumer choice. In the extreme, coverage gaps appear: insurers withdraw from certain geographies or triggers, and the lifeboat (the residual market) starts taking on water. None of this requires a stronger storm. It only requires a less predictable regime. Stability invites capital; improvisation taxes it.

Spectrum check: Stabilize the regime and spreads compress; destabilize it and portfolios reprice—or depart.

Catastrophe, Models, and the Modern Coastal Dilemma

In the late 20th century, hurricane catastrophes forced another leap forward. Advanced meteorology and probabilistic catastrophe models emerged to estimate frequency, severity, track, and surge. Modeling firms synthesized historical data, climate signals, vulnerability curves, occupancy types, and construction attributes to project loss distributions. For insurers and reinsurers, this was liberation: hurricane risk—though volatile—could be **modeled**. Pricing became more disciplined; capital flows followed those models.

But models have assumptions, and assumptions must be nested in **stable rules**. A model can absorb new weather data; it cannot absorb a midnight, retroactive change in litigation incentives, coverage triggers, or claims-handling statutes. In other words: models tame **risk**; they cannot domesticate **uncertainty**. This is where Florida's story diverges from the clean arc of "fate to formula."

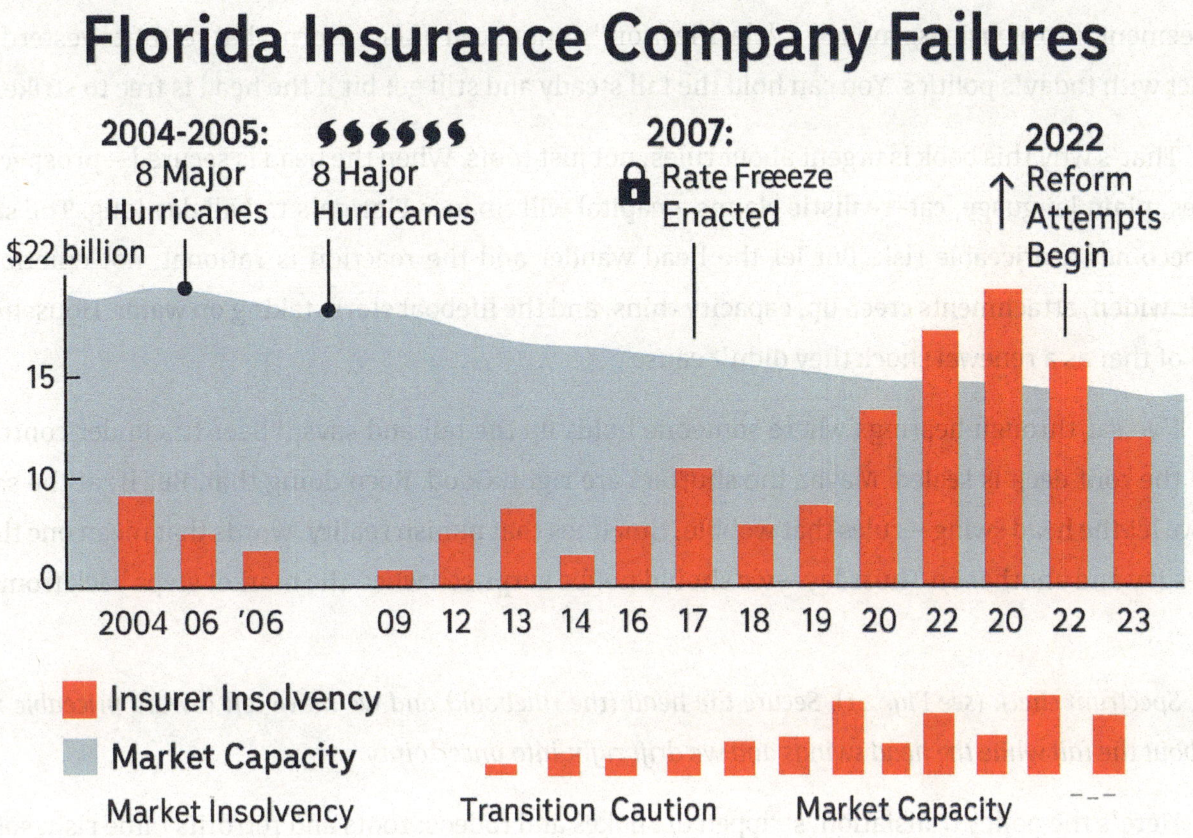

Figure 1 – The End of the Road and the Edge of the Map

Florida: The End of the Road and the Edge of the Map

Florida is where ancient principles meet modern exposure. The coastline is long, the population large, and the total insured value immense. Hurricanes are part of the bargain of living in paradise. And yet the real fragility of Florida's market is not meteorological; it is institutional.[6]

Let me put that difference in plain sight. We treat hurricanes like a threat because they're loud and visible. But markets don't run from **peril** they can measure; they run from **process** they can't predict. A quick story from my youth makes the point better than any chart.

My father used to work the rattlesnake rodeos. If you've never watched one, here's the only lesson that matters: you can grab a rattlesnake by the tail and look brave for a moment. Then the head finds you. It doesn't matter how tough you are, how fast your hands are, or how much the crowd cheers. If the **head** can still move, you're not in control.

Hurricanes are the tail—violent, yes, but visible and measured. We can glove up for them. We can model their behavior, set our stance, and buy protection. **Uncertainty is the head.** It's the end you don't see until it finds you: a clause that suddenly means something no underwriter priced; a fee rule that turns disagreement into a business model; a "clarification" announced after a storm that retrofits yesterday's contract with today's politics. You can hold the tail steady and still get bit if the head is free to strike.

That's why this book is urgent about rules, not just roofs. When the head is secured—**prospective** changes, **plain** language, **cat-realistic** claims—capital will finance Florida's tail all day long. The same wind becomes a priceable risk. But let the head wander and the reaction is rational, not emotional: spreads widen, attachments creep up, capacity thins, and the lifeboat starts taking on water. Households feel all of that as a renewal shock they didn't cause.

I've sat through hearings where someone holds up the tail and says, "See? It's under control." Maybe the roof deck is sealed. Maybe the shutters are right. Good. Keep doing that. But if, at the same time, we let the head swing—rules that wobble, timelines that punish reality, words that mean one thing on Tuesday and another on Thursday—we should not be surprised when the market steps back from the cage.

Spectrum check (see Fig. 2.1): Secure the head (the rulebook) and we move left toward priceable risk; brag about the tail while the head swings and we drift right into uncertainty.

Here's the policy translation, stripped of snakes and rodeos: roofs and retrofits tame **risk**; sober, **prospective** rules tame **uncertainty**. Affordability requires both. In the pages that follow we'll measure the risk side with the tools that deserve your trust—AALs, EP curves, rate-on-line—and we'll show how discipline on the rulebook side keeps those numbers honest. In **Chapter 2**, we'll formalize this as the **Risk–Uncertainty Spectrum** and use it to track whether our choices move Florida **left** (priceable risk) or **right** (uncertainty). That's the map capital reads—and the bill homeowners receive.

Florida Snapshot, 2017–2022: What Uncertainty Cost

Between 2017 and 2022, 19 insurers exited Florida or became insolvent, taking roughly $2.3 billion in capital off the field. That didn't happen because the wind changed; it happened because the rules did—through fee dynamics, retroactive readings, and operational mandates that didn't scale after landfall. Fewer carriers meant thinner competition and more stress on reinsurance placements—costs that later surfaced in renewal notices.

Spectrum check: Those exits reflect a rightward move on the Risk–Uncertainty Spectrum—same peril, less predictable regime.

Consider the homeowner in Miami, Punta Gorda, or Pensacola. She budgets carefully, saves, and pays her premium every year. She understands the risk of storms—she's boarded windows and set out sandbags before. What she cannot plan for is the **policy whiplash** that raises premiums sharply, expands or narrows coverage definitions, alters attorney-fee rules, or encourages behaviors that swell claim severity. For her, the storm outside is frightening; the storm **inside** the marketplace is bewildering.

Reinsurers and ILS investors feel the same. They accept hurricane risk because the loss distributions are (imperfectly) knowable. But they recoil from **shifting ground** in law and regulation because those shifts are not quantifiable. Capital is comfortable with wind and water; it is uncomfortable with ambiguity. When ambiguity rises, capital drains.

Humor in the History (Because Gravity Needs Levity)

Insurance may seem dry, but anyone who has tried to draw bright lines between risk and uncertainty knows the experience can feel like herding ducks—only to discover, mid-stride, that the ducks have started **quacking in a different language**. That's how markets feel when the legal environment changes after the fact.

And then there's the old Irish blessing: *"May those that love us—love us. And for those that don't, may God turn their heart. And for those whose hearts He cannot turn, may He turn their ankle—so that we will know them by their limping."* If only capital signaled its exit that clearly. In practice, it doesn't limp. It leaves. By the time homeowners notice, the market has already repriced, and the "limp" shows up as a renewal shock.

Humor does not trivialize the stakes; it humanizes them. It reminds us that behind every policy is a family, and behind every market rule is a set of incentives that either invite prudence or reward peril.

Price as a Compass, Not a Punishment

Price is not a moral judgment; it is a **signal**. In competitive markets, prices convey information about scarcity and risk. High prices in high-hazard zones are telling the truth: the expected cost of loss is elevated. When those signals are muted or distorted—by subsidies that ignore hazard, by legal structures that inflate loss costs—the compass spins. Builders erect where they shouldn't, homeowners under-invest in mitigation, and insurers either charge more or withdraw.

Accurate risk-based pricing does three socially valuable things: (1) it **alerts** people to hazard (risk awareness), (2) it **nudges** behavior toward safer construction and location (behavior modification), and (3) it **allocates** capital to resilience rather than to repetitive loss. That is as true today as it was in Babylon. The difference is scale: mispricing on a modern coastline can ripple through mortgage markets, municipal finances, and household budgets statewide.

This does not mean compassion is incompatible with pricing. It means compassion should be paired with **targeted aid** (for low-income, high-hazard households) and **pre-event investment** (hardening homes, upgrading codes) rather than blanket socialization of loss that erodes incentives and accelerates fragility.

Why This Distinction Matters for You

This isn't an academic parlor trick. For a homeowner, the risk–uncertainty line explains why shutters, a sealed roof deck, and a reinforced garage door reliably reduce price over time—risk moves left when loss shrinks. It also explains why, despite those upgrades, a renewal can still jump after a quiet year—uncertainty moved right because the rulebook did. For agents, the line is a translation tool: it separates "wind got worse" from "process got fuzzy." For investors and reinsurers, it's the difference between pricing a peril and declining a jurisdiction. Your family budget, your carrier's solvency, and your state's reputation with capital all trace back to this line. Keep the cards face up and the ducks quacking in the same language, and markets will finance your wind. Shuffle the deck mid-hand, and they won't.

Spectrum check: Household actions attack risk; policy discipline attacks uncertainty. Affordability needs both.

Mutual Aid, Moral Hazard, and the Human Factor

From the collegia to Lloyd's syndicates to today's residual markets, risk sharing is a social triumph. But it always carries a shadow: **moral hazard**. When people are insulated from the consequences of their choices, they may take on more risk. If we promise to rebuild the same vulnerable structures over and over—without asking for stronger roofs, higher elevations, or wiser siting—then we are not sharing risk; we are **manufacturing** it.

The solution is not to abandon solidarity. It is to align solidarity with **incentives**: premium credits for fortified roofs, grants for shutters and elevation, streamlined permitting for retrofits, mitigation loans repaid on the tax bill, and disclosure rules that help buyers see flood and wind history clearly. In short: protect people, but insist on progress.[7]

Prevention as Policy: From Fire Marks to Fortified Homes

After the Great Fire of London, policyholders affixed metal **fire marks** to their buildings so private brigades would know whom to save first. The symbolism endures: prevention and insurance are two sides of the same coin. Today, the analogues are **building codes**, **retrofit programs**, and **parcel-level mitigation**—not as political slogans, but as risk-costing, premium-lowering, claim-reducing engines of stability.

Florida's future affordability depends less on post-event bailouts and more on **pre-event fortification**: roof decks that hold, gable ends that don't fail, garage doors that don't blow in, elevation where feasible, and strategic retreat were not. Every dollar spent on resilience before landfall saves multiples after—and, crucially, makes the state **insurable** at all.

Reinsurance: The Shock Absorber with Memory

Reinsurance is the market's shock absorber. In good years, it looks like a cost center. In bad years, it looks like salvation. But reinsurers have long memories and global options. If a jurisdiction chronically converts risk into uncertainty—if loss costs are amplified by legal volatility rather than by hazard—reinsurance capacity will contract or demand higher price and tighter terms. That is not vindictiveness; it is arithmetic.

Conversely, when a jurisdiction steadily reduces uncertainty—clarifies statutes, streamlines claims resolution, deters abuse, strengthens codes, funds mitigation—capacity expands, terms soften, and consumers ultimately benefit. Stability is not an abstraction; it is a premium line item.

A Florida Vignette: Maria's Two Storms

Meet Maria, a school administrator in Fort Myers. She knows the ritual: stock water, board windows, call her mother inland. She pays for wind coverage every year and keeps photos of the house for claims. The hurricane is terrifying, but it is a storm she understands.

The second storm arrives at renewal. Her premium leaps by thousands. Her neighbor's carrier non-renews. Citizens grows. She calls her agent, who explains changes in the reinsurance market and in the legal environment. Maria realizes there are **two** storms to plan for: the one on the radar, and the one in statute. She can buy shutters for the first. For the second, she can only hope policymakers keep their hands steady on the wheel.[8]

This is not an abstract complaint. It is the lived experience of households across the state—and it is precisely what divides **risk** from **uncertainty**. Maria can prepare for a hurricane. She cannot prepare for rules that change after she has paid her premium.

Rhetorical Interlude: Questions We Must Ask

- If price is a signal, what happens when we silence it?
- If solidarity is the goal, why not fund it **before** the storm by hardening homes, rather than **after**, by socializing losses?
- If capital is mobile, what persuades it to stay—heroism in disaster, or humility in policymaking?

- If we know which roofs fail, which doors blow in, which neighborhoods flood, why are we debating whether mitigation "pays"? (It does. The only real question is **who** pays and **when**.)

These are not ideological questions. They are engineering, economics, and ethics braided together. They will surface in every chapter that follows.

The Economics of Pooling: Why Large Numbers Matter

Behind the history lies arithmetic. The **Law of Large Numbers** says that as you pool many independent risks, the average loss becomes more predictable. Variance shrinks relative to the mean. That is why a statewide or regional pool can price loss better than a single household can, and why reinsurance—pooling across states and countries—stabilizes results further still. The catch is in the word **independent**. When losses are highly correlated—when many roofs in the same county fail at once—the law works more slowly and more expensively.

Correlation also explains why mitigation pays twice: it lowers expected loss **and** lowers correlation. A fortified roof not only resists wind; it reduces the chance that a whole neighborhood fails simultaneously. Markets will pay for that. They will reward lower tail risk with lower prices, but only if the signal is allowed to pass through the system without distortion.

Global Comparators: Learning From Others

Florida is not alone in facing catastrophe. The **Caribbean Catastrophe Risk Insurance Facility (CCRIF)** allows small island nations to buy parametric coverage that pays quickly after hurricanes and earthquakes. The United Kingdom's **Flood Re** scheme helps households in high-risk flood zones obtain cover while nudging builders and councils toward better land-use choices. Japan's earthquake reinsurance system shares losses between private insurers and the government according to predefined layers. The designs differ, but the thread is the same: clarity about who pays, when, and how much.

The lesson for Florida is not to copy and paste another model, but to imitate the virtue of **predictability**. Markets will accept high hazard. They balk at changing rules.

Florida's Family Album of Storms

Scan Florida's historical record and you see a rhythm: years of quiet punctuated by brutal seasons. Each era has left fingerprints on the market. Major landfalls revealed weak building practices; subsequent reforms reduced some vulnerabilities; economic booms drew more people to the coast; and new legal incentives occasionally amplified losses beyond what wind alone would have caused. The details change; the pattern does not. Resilience grows when experience is translated into stronger standards and steady policy—when we remember, not just rebuild.

That is why the stories in this book are not mere anecdotes. They are evidence of how human choices interact with natural hazard. Where codes strengthened roofs, claims fell. Where shortcuts were tolerated, losses compounded. Where rules were predictable, capital returned. Where uncertainty grew, it left.

What the Long Road Teaches Policymakers

History does not hand us a script, but it does hand us guardrails: price risk honestly; invest in prevention early; make the rules clear and give markets time to adjust; protect the vulnerable with targeted help, not with blank checks that erode incentives. Above all, resist the temptation to solve a 20-year problem with a 20-day fix. A durable insurance market is not built with adrenaline. It is built with patience and principle.

Case Study in Incentives: From London's Fire to Florida's Roofs

After 1666, Londoners did something profound: they rebuilt differently. Timber frames gave way to brick and stone, jettied upper stories disappeared, and narrow alleys were widened to break fire pathways. Insurers priced these improvements into premiums and, by doing so, accelerated safer rebuilding. Price sent a message; builders received it; the city became safer and more insurable.

Florida has the same lever at hand. When underwriting recognizes **Fortified** standards, secondary water barriers, ring-shank nails, and continuous load paths, the signal reaches the jobsite; contractors install what the contract pays for.

Consider a simple thought experiment. Two otherwise identical houses sit side-by-side on the same street. One has a strapped roof, a reinforced garage door, and window protection; the other does not. If both pay the same premium, the careful owner subsidizes the careless. If the fortified home pays less, the neighbor has a reason to upgrade. Multiply that decision by a million households and you have policy that **compounds resilience** instead of fragility. Markets work when they are allowed to communicate risk honestly through price and coverage, and when households are equipped to respond.

A Plainspoken Bridge to Chapter 2

This chapter has argued that insurance is a civilizational tool: it turns chance into choice. But the tool has limits. It works on **risk**—things we can model and price—even when those things are violent and rare. It fails on **uncertainty**—the human tendency to change rules after the dice have rolled. Florida sits with one foot in each world. The wind is risk. The whiplash is uncertainty.

In Chapter 2, we pick up Frank Knight's compass. We will use it to read the map of Florida's market so that homeowners, builders, and lawmakers can see which choices attract capital and which repel it.

Closing Thought: The Courage to Be Predictable

"Courage" in public life is often confused with dramatic gestures. In catastrophe insurance, courage looks plainer: **predictability**. It is the courage to let prices signal risk even when the signals are unpopular; the courage to invest in mitigation before the headline; the courage to enforce codes evenly; the courage to say **no** to short-term applause when it would buy long-term instability. The market does not demand perfection. It demands a fair game played by clear rules.

That was true in Babylon; it is true in Florida.

Key Terms Primer (for the General Reader)

- **Risk**: A hazard with estimable probabilities and loss distributions; insurable through pricing, pooling, and capital markets.
- **Uncertainty**: Hazards or outcomes with unknown or unstable probabilities; not reliably insurable because models cannot calibrate them.
- **Moral Hazard**: When protection against loss encourages riskier behavior, raising total losses unless incentives are corrected.
- **Mitigation**: Physical measures that reduce loss severity (e.g., roof decking, shutters, elevation); lowers premiums when priced.
- **Reinsurance/ILS**: Contracts and securities that spread catastrophe risk globally so local markets remain solvent after big events.

One-Page Summary

Insurance is mankind's oldest resilience technology. From Hammurabi to Franklin to modern reinsurers, its genius is turning devastating losses into shared, predictable costs. That genius fails when rules shift after the fact. Florida's hazard is storms; its fragility is uncertainty. If we price risk honestly, invest in mitigation, align incentives, and keep the legal ground steady, capital will stay, premiums will stabilize, and families will be safer. If we don't, the capital drain will continue—and no amount of post-storm subsidy will substitute for the confidence that only predictability can buy.

Sidebar: Key Terms Primer

A quick, plain-English primer you can scan now and skip looking up later.

Risk vs. Uncertainty — Risk has knowable (even estimated) odds; uncertainty does not. Markets price risk; they flee uncertainty.

Ambiguity Aversion — Human tendency to prefer known odds over unknown odds (Ellsberg's jellybean problem).

Average Annual Loss (AAL) — Long-run expected loss from a peril in a typical year—the "rent" you pay to live with the risk.[9]

EP Curve (Exceedance Probability) — The chance that losses exceed a threshold (e.g., 1-in-100 year); committees watch the tail.

Tail Value at Risk (TVaR) — Average loss once you're already in a severe tail—what strains solvency.[10]

Rate on Line (ROL) — Reinsurance shorthand: premium divided by limit for an excess layer.

Attachment / Exhaustion — Where a reinsurance layer starts paying and where it maxes out.

Catastrophe Bond (Cat Bond) — A bond that forfeits principal if a specified catastrophe trigger is met; clear structure brings capital markets in.

Parametric Trigger — Pays based on a measured parameter (wind speed, pressure) rather than indemnity; clear but introduces basis risk.

Basis Risk — Mismatch between contract payout and actual loss—can be positive or negative.

Trapped Collateral — Investor funds frozen post-event while losses are resolved; raises demanded spreads next season.[11]

Coverage Creep — Post-event interpretation expands what a policy must pay beyond what was priced.

Prospective vs. Retroactive — Prospective rules apply going forward; retroactive changes reach back to policies already priced and sold.

Residual Market — Public insurer of last resort; must be solvent, transparent, and visibly rowing back to private markets.

Mitigation Credits — Material premium reductions for verified features (sealed deck, opening protection, reinforced garage door).

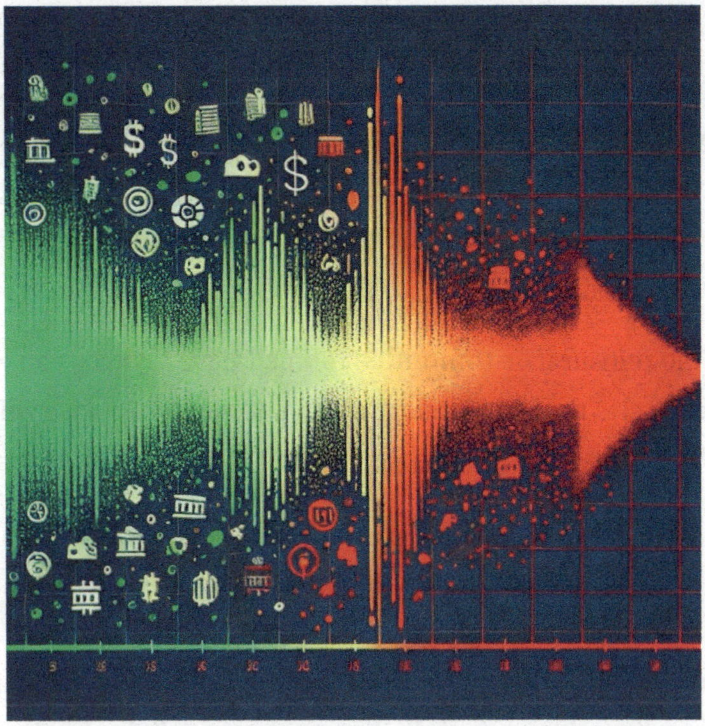

Chapter 2 – Knight's Warning: Risk vs. Uncertainty

The Line That Saves Markets

Economics has few ideas that deserve a banner across the top of the page. This is one of them. **Risk can be priced. Uncertainty cannot.** Risk has odds—even if they're messy. Uncertainty does not. If we honor that line, capital behaves. If we blur it, capital bolts.

I didn't learn this in a classroom. I learned it watching what happens when a storm hits and the rulebook trembles. Hurricanes are brutal, but they are **risk**—measurable, modelable, reinsurable. Their violence can be converted into numbers a balance sheet can carry. Uncertainty is different. It is the midnight surprise that says a clause means what no one thought it meant. It is the fee rule that turns a disagreement into a business model. It is the retroactive gesture that feels merciful at the microphone and murderous in the model.

The difference fits on a single line I keep in my head—a **spectrum**. On the far left lives the kind of risk insurers love: well-defined hazards with deep data and stable rules. Think well-built houses under a modern code, priced with updated loss curves and backed by plain contracts. Slide a little to the right and the data thin, the structures vary, the models need judgment. Still risk. Still priceable. Move further right and the hazard remains the same but the **regime**—law, procedure, incentives—starts to wobble. This is the dangerous middle: the wind looks familiar; the process does not. One more step and you fall off the map. That's **uncertainty**. When the probabilities themselves are unknowable or change mid-game, models turn from instruments into decorations. The only rational response is retreat.

Every storm season re-draws this spectrum. Not the wind—the rules. With each statute, court decision, or operational edict, we nudge entire portfolios left toward risk or right toward uncertainty. That nudge is invisible to the homeowner boarding windows on a Thursday night. It becomes very visible on the renewal that arrives six months later.

If you could sit in the reinsurance committee rooms I have visited, you would see the spectrum taped to the wall. A partner circles the left side with a pen and says, "This we will fund all day." He taps the right edge and says, "This we won't touch at any price." What separates the two isn't courage. It's **clarity**.

I carry one more picture that keeps me honest when the easy answers tempt. Imagine two jars of jellybeans. In one, the ratio is 50-50, clearly labeled. In the other, the colors are concealed. The first jar is **risk**. The second jar is **uncertainty**. We all say we're bold until the hand hovers over the covered jar. Then most of us discover we are prudent after all. Investors are no different. They will finance our wind if we show them the beans. They will not if we insist on covering the jar and calling it compassion.

So here is the center of this chapter and, in a real sense, the center of this book: **good policy moves exposures left on the spectrum.** It turns ambiguity into measurable risk—by writing rules prospectively, by drafting precisely, by designing claims for catastrophe reality, and by making mitigation the cheapest habit in the state. Bad policy does the opposite. It pushes us right, then pretends surprise when capacity leaves.

If you remember nothing else, remember the line. Remember that premiums rise fastest when the market is asked to price what cannot be priced. Remember that homeowners pay for uncertainty twice—once in the check they write today and again in the capacity that does not show up tomorrow. Remember, most of all, that we control more of this spectrum than we think. The wind is the wind. The rulebook is ours.

Turn the page. I want you to see the picture I keep in my head.

Figure 2.1 — The Risk-Uncertainty Spectrum

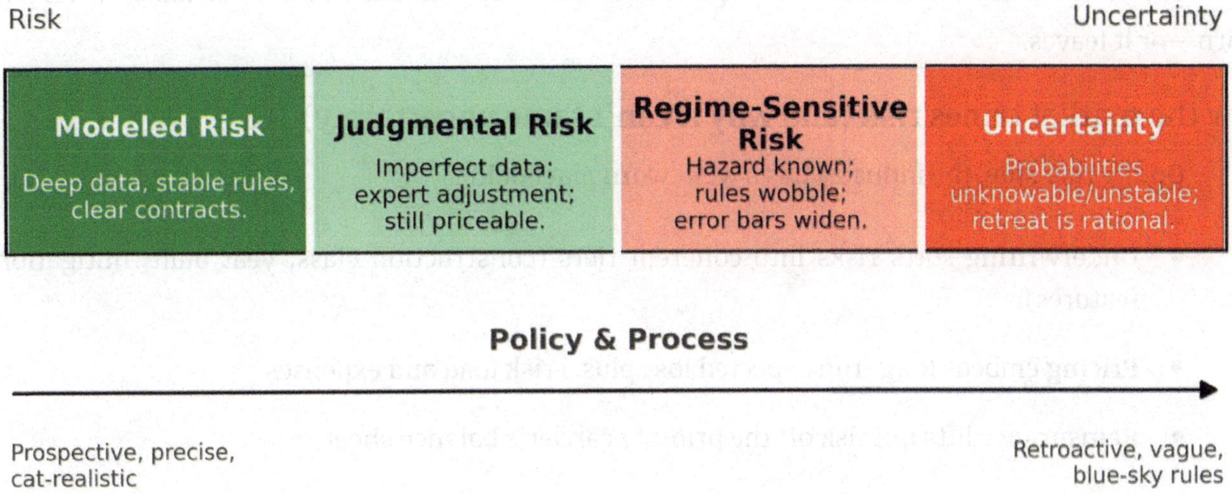

Insurance thrives on the left, where hazards are measurable and rules are steady. As legal and operational regimes wobble, the same wind migrates right: variance fattens, models lose traction, and required returns jump. Good policy moves exposures left-turning ambiguity into priceable risk.

Hurricanes: calculable chaos

Make no mistake: hurricanes are brutal. But they are also **modelable**. Flood maps, track probabilities, intensity distributions, construction-class vulnerabilities, secondary modifiers (roof decks, garage doors, shutters)—all of these pour into catastrophe models that project long-run expected loss. Those projections are noisy and imperfect, but they're coherent enough for pricing, underwriting, and portfolio management.

This is why billions have flowed into reinsurance and insurance-linked securities over the past two decades. Investors do not love losing money—no one does—but they accept that a priced, probabilistic peril can pay over time. The discipline of modeling and diversification turns terrifying storms into something a balance sheet can bear.

Uncertainty: the angry bear rowing your boat backward

Uncertainty is different. It is the event you didn't model because you couldn't—**the angry bear that jumps into your canoe and starts rowing you backward**

No peril catalog includes "surprise fee multiplier," "overnight coverage expansion," or "retroactive rule change." Those are human inventions, and they explode loss costs in ways no wind field ever could.

Try to price that. You can't. So, capital does the only rational thing: it demands a very high return—or it leaves.

How the market tames risk (and why it can't tame uncertainty)

On the risk side, the industry has a well-worn playbook:

- **Underwriting** sorts risks into coherent tiers (construction class, year built, mitigation features).
- **Pricing** embeds long-run expected loss plus a risk load and expenses.
- **Reinsurance** lifts tail risk off the primary carrier's balance sheet.
- **Capital markets** take a further slice through cat bonds and collateralized reinsurance. [12]
- **Mitigation and codes** gradually reduce expected loss and variance, which filters back into lower rates.

On the uncertainty side, there is no comparable tool. You can't reinsure ambiguity. You can't securitize a shifting rulebook. You can only sidestep it: write less, charge more, or redeploy capital elsewhere.

Transmission mechanisms: how risk becomes uncertainty

Uncertainty doesn't appear out of thin air; it gets **transmitted** through specific channels:

1. **Coverage creep**: Ambiguous policy language is reinterpreted broadly after a loss wave. Premiums priced for one contract suddenly fund a larger one.
1. **Litigation incentives**: Fee-shifting structures or assignment mechanics turn routine disagreements into systemic severity.
2. **Retroactivity**: Rules applied to already-bound policies transform yesterday's risk into today's uncertainty.
3. **Operational chokepoints**: Claims protocols or timelines that cannot be met at catastrophe scale convert good-faith operations into penalties.
4. **Residual market policy churn**: When the plan of last resort becomes the largest writer, private capacity reads the signal: uncertainty ahead.

Each mechanism erodes the model's connection to reality. And when models stop describing reality, capital stops listening to models.

The "concert effect": Beethoven, not jazz (mid-symphony)

Think of an insurance market like a symphony. You bought a ticket to Beethoven's Fifth; there may be squeaks, but the score is known. That's risk. Imagine, mid-movement, the conductor announces: *We're switching to improvisational jazz.* Some will enjoy the surprise. Investors will head for the exits. They priced Beethoven, not bebop. The music changed; so, did the contract between stage and audience.

Markets do not resist all change—they resist **surprise**. Stability is not stasis; it's **predictable evolution.**

A day in the life: how decisions get made when the rulebook wobbles

The Underwriter: Building a renewal portfolio for a coastal county, she's comfortable walking close to the edge—if the edge is charted. A late-session statutory tweak shifts attorney fees and discovery rules. Her expected-loss curve balloons on the severe tail. Submission appetite shrinks; deductibles and prices rise. Not out of spite—out of arithmetic.

The Reinsurance Committee: Reviewing Florida layers, they ask two questions: *How did the wind behave? How did the law behave?* The first answer comes from models; the second from newspapers and counsel. If the second answer reads "volatile," capital deployment tightens. That's not ideology; that's fiduciary duty.

The Homeowner: She did the right things—strapped roof, shutters, a clean inspection. But her renewal still jumps. Why? Because she is not just paying for *her* risk; she is paying for **systemic uncertainty** that her carrier and reinsurers must now price into everyone's bill.

The Regulator: Charged with consumer protection and solvency, the regulator knows predictability serves both. Pre-announced, non-retroactive changes are digestible. Retroactive improvisation isn't. The art is balancing pace and clarity—signal early, implement cleanly, and let markets adjust.

Behavioral economics: why ambiguity aversion multiplies the damage

Even if the modeled risk and the unmodeled uncertainty had the same expected loss, investors would still prefer the modeled peril. That is **ambiguity aversion**—the Ellsberg intuition we'll explore in the next chapter. Add **loss aversion** (losses hurt more than equivalent gains please) and **herding** (capital follows capacity leaders), and you get a simple rule of thumb: **the market punishes uncertainty twice**—once for the expected loss, and again for the unknowns around it.

That double punishment shows up in higher required returns, tighter terms, and, sometimes, a hard pass.

Price is the messenger; don't shoot it

When uncertainty rises, **price** is the first messenger to arrive. It is telling the truth—about tail risk, frictional severity, and the cost of capital. If we silence the messenger (via blunt suppression), we don't make risk cheaper; we push capacity away and push volatility onto taxpayers and future buyers. If, instead, we **decode** the message, it points to solutions: clearer rules, cleaner contracts, stronger mitigation, and non-retroactive reforms that invite capital back.

Price is not punishment. In competitive markets, it is information.

Capital Response (How Committees Actually Behave by Zone)

Green → Scale the program; accept slightly tighter spreads next season if performance holds.

Light green → Participate within risk limits; monitor legal trend; size cautiously.

Light red → Increase spread, push attachments up, add protective wordings and hours clauses.

Dark red → Stand back. Re-enter only on clear, prospective reforms with visible runway.

Spectrum check: Capital does not get braver; it gets comparative. Unknown odds lose to known cash yields every time.

"Aces and eights": when to play, when to fold

I have muttered at my desk more than once, "Risk vs. uncertainty—if that ain't a pair of aces and eights, I don't know what is."

In poker, wisdom is knowing when to press and when to walk. Florida's challenge is to play the strong hands (modelable risk, code-driven mitigation, pre-event finance) and fold the losers (retroactive improvisation, incentives that explode severity, uncertainty that no premium can carry).

What predictability actually looks like (a practical checklist)

Predictability is not an abstraction; it's a **design choice**. Here's a market-tested checklist:

1. **Non-retroactivity as a rule of life**: Apply statutory and regulatory changes prospectively. Yesterday's price cannot fund today's surprise.
2. **Advance signaling**: Publish exposure drafts, hold technical hearings, and announce effective dates far enough out that carriers and reinsurers can price for change.
3. **Clarity beats poetry**: Draft coverage and fee rules in plain, bounded language. Precision now is cheaper than litigation later.

4. **Operational realism**: Align claims timelines and documentation standards with catastrophe reality; don't turn surge into procedural default.
5. **Mitigation first**: Tie meaningful premium credits and grant programs to verifiable, loss-reducing upgrades (roof decks, openings, garage doors, elevation).
6. **Data feedback loops**: Require anonymized loss-and-litigation reporting so reforms can be tuned based on observed effects, not anecdotes.
7. **Residual market guardrails**: Keep last-resort plans solvent, fairly priced, and on a glidepath back to private markets as stability returns.
8. **Contract certainty**: Encourage clearer forms and rapid dispute resolution (appraisal, mediation) to keep disagreements from metastasizing into systemic severity.
9. **Cat finance hygiene**: Use pre-event financing (reinsurance, cat bonds, resilient reserves) rather than post-event debt where possible; the former is almost always cheaper than the latter over time.
10. **Sunset and review**: Every major change should sunset or be reviewed on schedule. Markets adjust best to rules that are tested, not immortal.

Adopt even half of this, and capacity notices. Adopt most of it, and capacity returns.

Why mitigation is the market's love language

Capital is attracted to **risk it can see shrinking**. That's what mitigation does. A strapped roof, a sealed deck, protected openings, and a reinforced garage door don't just reduce expected loss; they reduce **correlation**—the chance that an entire neighborhood fails at once. Lower correlation means thinner tails; thinner tails mean cheaper reinsurance; cheaper reinsurance filters down to lower homeowner premiums.

It is not charity to subsidize mitigation for vulnerable households. It is finance: one-time upgrades beat permanent crisis pricing.

Preparedness Instruments: Buying Mercy Upstream

The Household Bridge (What Families Can Actually Do)

Policy can move the dot, but the house still meets the wind. The cheapest durable affordability is still earned on the ladder: a sealed deck, opening protection, and a reinforced garage door. When those features are verified and credibly credited, homeowners see the line move left in their own mailbox—not because anyone blinked at the bill, but because expected loss actually fell.

Spectrum check: Roof by roof, loss falls; statute by statute, uncertainty shrinks. That is how affordability compounds.

A brief detour to Babylon (because the ancients were onto something)

The oldest forms of insurance—guild funds, bottomry, and mutual aid—worked because everyone understood the terms and the community enforced them. The **Code of Hammurabi**'s proto-insurance clause only worked because it was carved in stone—known, stable, trusted

Random Excerpts from Previous W...

. The lesson isn't nostalgia; it's **design**. The more today's rules feel "carved in stone"—clear, pre-announced, non-retroactive—the more today's markets behave like those early mutuals: resilient, patient, and affordable.

Two storms, one decision

Picture a reinsurer with $1 billion to deploy. Portfolio A: a region with higher hurricane frequency but a stable legal regime and focused mitigation. Portfolio B: a region with similar hazard but a history of abrupt, retroactive legal shocks. Where does the capital go? To Portfolio A, every time, even if its modeled losses are slightly higher. That is Knight in action. That is ambiguity aversion in money, not words.

Florida's goal isn't to eliminate storms; it's to look like Portfolio A.

Rhetorical gut-checks for policymakers and market leaders

- If we can't price it today, why are we trying to pay it tomorrow?
- If a rule is good, why would we need to make it retroactive?
- If mitigation demonstrably lowers loss, why isn't every public dollar aimed at it before landfall?
- If residual markets grow, what is the exit plan—and is it credible enough for private capital to believe?

These are not trick questions. They are the difference between a market that compounds stability and one that compounds distress.

When uncertainty masquerades as compassion

There is a temptation, after a hard season, to deliver relief by bending the rulebook. The intention is humane. The effect can be corrosive. If relief arrives via uncertainty—retroactive coverage, procedural shortcuts that metastasize into systemic severity—future buyers pay for today's kindness with tomorrow's unaffordability. If, instead, relief arrives via **targeted, transparent subsidies** and **front-loaded resilience**, the compassion lands without destabilizing the pool.

Short-term applause is easy. Long-term affordability is leadership.

The Maria test (revisited)

Maria can budget for a known hurricane season. She cannot budget for unknown legal seasons. When we reduce uncertainty, we are not only stabilizing carriers and reinsurers; we are stabilizing Maria's household. That is why non-retroactivity and clarity are not "industry favors." They are **consumer protection** in their most durable form.

Humor, because gravity needs levity

At the risk of repeating myself: it all felt orderly—until the ducks started quacking in a different language

Random Excerpts from Previous W...

. And on a few long nights I have sighed, "Risk versus uncertainty—aces and eights," and pushed back from the desk

Random Excerpts from Previous W...

. The humor is not flippant. It's a reminder that economics is performed by humans with roofs, families, and bills. We owe them a market that is boring in the best way: predictable, durable, explainable.

A principle-based close: courage as predictability

The bravest act in catastrophe insurance is not bravura; it is **predictability**. It is the courage to:

- Let prices tell the truth about hazard.
- Fund resilience before landfall.
- Write clear rules and let them stand.
- Resist retroactivity, however tempting in the news cycle.
- Measure results and tune policy with humility, not pride.
- Knight drew the line. Our task is to stay on the right side of it.

Moving Left

Markets don't ask us to calm the wind. They ask us to move the dot. Roof by roof, statute by statute, season by season, we can slide Florida left across the spectrum. A sealed deck, strapped trusses, a reinforced garage door—each is a small nudge left. A plain sentence that means tomorrow what it means today—another nudge. A claims protocol that assumes the power will be out and the roads will be jammed—another. A refusal to reach backward with rules written in the heat of a headline—another. Add enough nudges and something quiet happens: spreads compress, placements place, and the renewal feels less like a referendum on our last argument and more like a price for wind.

I have sat in rooms where people call this boring. Good. Boring is solvency's lullaby. The spectrum rewards boredom—predictability disguised as prudence. It punishes improvisation—surprise disguised as compassion. We will always have storms. We can decide, together, where on this line we want to live when they arrive.

Bridge to Chapter 3: Jellybeans and judgment

We've treated Knight's theory as the backbone of market stability. In **Chapter 3**, we'll add the psychology: why, when faced with a jar of known odds and a jar of unknown odds, investors almost always choose the first—and why Florida's goal must be to look, feel, and price like the jar with known odds. In other words: turn ambiguity into risk, and capital into commitment.

Chapter 3 – The Ellsberg Paradox and the Jellybeans

What if the problem isn't hurricanes at all? What if the real storm is a jar of jellybeans with an unknown mix of colors—and your retirement, your mortgage, and your state's insurance market depend on whether investors feel like reaching into that jar? That, in plain language, is the Ellsberg Paradox, and it explains why global capital will fund Florida's wind but balk at Florida's whiplash. Hurricanes are violent; ambiguity is corrosive. Markets can shoulder the first. They flee the second.

The Paradox in a Handful of Candy

Daniel Ellsberg proposed a simple thought experiment. Place two jars on a table. Jar A holds exactly 100 jellybeans: 50 red, 50 black. Jar B also holds 100, but the mix is unknown. You may bet on drawing red from either jar. Most people choose Jar A, the one with known odds, even though Jar B could, in theory, be 99 red. This robust preference for the known over the unknown is called **ambiguity aversion.** It is distinct from **risk aversion**.

Poker with Cards vs. Poker in the Dark

Ellsberg tells us why we reach for the jar with visible odds. Poker tells us what happens when the odds go missing. Sit at a table where the deck is clean, the cards are face up, and the rules are fixed. You may be risk-averse—you don't shove all-in lightly—but you can price the risk. Now imagine a second table. The dealer might swap decks mid-hand. The meaning of a straight could change after the flop. You're still asked to ante. That isn't poker; that's theater. And prudent people don't fund theater with their retirement money.

Markets feel the same way. A Florida wind layer with clear wordings and stable claim practice is poker with cards—volatile, yes, but intelligible. A layer written under statutes that wobble, fee rules that multiply after landfall, or retroactive reinterpretations of coverage is poker in the dark. Investment committees don't argue about **how much** to bet at that table; they argue about **whether** to sit down at all. Most don't. Not because they're timid, but because you can't hedge a rule that can change after you've paid.

This is the investor's version of Ellsberg's insight. People accept known risk at a fair price. They'll even accept ugly volatility if the game is fixed in advance. What they won't accept is **unknown** odds or **movable** odds. That's why the job of policy isn't to make hurricanes gentle; it is to keep the cards face up. Write rules prospectively. Draft narrowly and plainly. Design claims for catastrophe reality. Do those three things and capital will sit down again—cautious, priced, and present when the wind arrives.

Spectrum check (see Fig. 2.1): Poker with cards keeps us **left** on the spectrum (priceable risk); poker in the dark pushes us **right** (uncertainty).

Ambiguity Aversion vs. Risk Aversion (Why the Distinction Matters)

The distinction matters because it shapes price, appetite, and the structure of deals.

Risk aversion can be managed with price and diversification. If a reinsurer is risk-averse, you offer a higher expected return, layer the risk so tail losses are bounded, and diversify across regions and perils. The probability distribution is known (or estimated), so the reinsurer can calibrate exposure.

Ambiguity aversion resists price. If the distribution itself is unknown—because courts, statutes, or administrative rules can change the payoff after premiums are collected—no premium is "high enough," because the **support** of the distribution is undefined. You don't know how bad "bad" can get. Faced with that, capital often imposes an **ambiguity haircut** (a catch-all margin) or, more often, simply exits.

Think of the haircut as an "uncertainty toll" layered on top of normal risk loadings. Homeowners never see a line item labeled "toll for ambiguity," but they feel it—in diminished availability, stricter terms, and sharp renewal jumps after legal shocks.

From Jellybeans to Catastrophe Bonds: How Investors Actually Decide

Let's translate candy jars into an investment committee memo.

Deal 1 (Jar A, known odds): A Florida indemnity catastrophe bond attaches at a 1-in-20 annual probability (5%) and exhausts at 1-in-40 (2.5% exceedance probability for full exhaustion), with a modeled expected loss of 3.25% and a proposed spread of 8.5% over risk-free. Triggers are clear, wordings are standard, and there have been no recent retroactive coverage shifts.

Deal 2 (Jar B, unknown odds): An otherwise similar bond, but the jurisdiction has a recent history of surprise fee multipliers, broadened coverage interpretations, and post-event rule changes that shifted loss costs outside the modeled envelope. Modeled expected loss is still shown as 3.25%, but the investor doubts the model's perimeter because the legal environment has moved unpredictably in prior seasons.

What happens in committee? For Deal 1, the debate is about price vs. model confidence. For Deal 2, the debate collapses to a binary: **participate or abstain**. No spreadsheet can conjure a stable probability distribution from unstable rules. The rational outcome is either a very high required spread (which often makes the deal uneconomic for the sponsor) or a pass.

This is Ellsberg at work: investors choose the jar with known odds—even if it pays less—because they can size, hedge, and justify the risk.

Anatomy of Ambiguity: Where It Enters the System

Ambiguity does not float in from the Gulf of Mexico. It enters through human systems. The common gateways:

1. **Coverage Creep.** Post-event reinterpretations of policy language transform a contract priced for X into a contract obliged to pay X+Y. Models priced X; capital finds itself funding Y. That delta is ambiguity realized.

2. **Fee Dynamics.** One-way fee regimes, multiplier doctrines, or incentives that reward protraction turn friction into severity. Severity inflation that depends on litigation behavior is hard to model ex ante.[13]

3. **Retroactivity.** Rules that reach backward—changing obligations for policies already bound—convert yesterday's priced risk into today's unpriced liability.

4. **Operational Unrealism.** Claims timelines, documentation rules, or penalty structures that fail at catastrophe scale can transmogrify ordinary claims handling into systemic legal exposure.

5. **Residual Market Distortion.** When the insurer of last resort grows too large, private markets infer that political constraints—not economics—will drive pricing and claims policy. That inference raises the ambiguity toll for everyone.

None of these are meteorology. All are **institutional**. That's why ambiguity is solvable with policy discipline—and why it recurs when discipline lapses.

When the Ducks Change Languages

There's a joke investors tell when a jurisdiction rewrites the rulebook after a storm: "The ducks started quacking in a different language." Everyone laughs, because that's what uncertainty sounds like in real time—familiar shapes making unfamiliar noises. One week, "appraisal" means appraisal; the next, a fee rule turns it into trench warfare. One week, "roof damage" means the policy definition; the next, a creative reading stretches it to the fence line. The wind didn't change. The *quacks* did.

Humor aside, that noise is expensive. It fattens tails, traps collateral, and pushes allocations toward places where the ducks still quack in English—where words mean tomorrow what they mean today. Keep the quacks consistent and capital stays; let them shift and the room gets quiet at renewal. The cure is not brave speeches. It's boring discipline: prospective change only, plain language, and claims protocols that assume the grid will be down and tempers up. Do that, and even when the pond is choppy, the ducks sound the same—and money keeps swimming.

Spectrum check (see Fig. 2.1): Stable "quacks" keep exposures **left**; shifting definitions push portfolios **right**.

A Stylized Decomposition of Premium (Where Ambiguity Hides)

For a coastal homeowner, the annual premium can be thought of—stylized, not literal—as:

Premium ≈ Expected Loss (wind, surge) + Expense Load + Risk Load (capital cost) + Reinsurance Cost + Ambiguity Load.

- The **Expected Loss** component is what catastrophe models estimate.
- The **Expense Load** pays for distribution and claims infrastructure.
- The **Risk Load** compensates capital for bearing volatility at known probabilities.
- **Reinsurance Cost** is the price of transferring tail risk to global markets.
- The **Ambiguity Load** is what swells when rules shift. It is not a formal line item; it is the shadow that lengthens every other line: reinsurers demand more, risk loads inflate, capacity shrinks, and non-rate terms tighten.

When a policymaker says "we didn't change the hazard, so why did premiums rise?", the answer is often that the **Ambiguity Load** rose—even as the hurricane peril stayed the same.

Behavioral Economics: Why the Unknown Punishes Twice

Three behavioral dynamics magnify ambiguity's cost:

- **Ambiguity Aversion.** Investors discount payoffs when the odds are unknown, demanding higher yields or refusing to play. That discount is not linear; it can jump at thresholds when rule instability crosses a confidence boundary.
- **Loss Aversion.** Losses loom larger than gains. After a surprise legal loss wave, committees overweight the recent worst case, raising required spreads more than models suggest.
- **Career Risk & Herding.** Investment managers fear being "wrong alone." If a jurisdiction's rules look unstable, it is safer—career-wise—to underweight or avoid than to defend a contrarian allocation. The first few exits become a stampede.

These dynamics are human, persistent, and predictable. They are not corrected by lecturing markets; they are calmed by **making the jar look like Jar A again**—clear, bounded, credible.

Cat Finance 101: Where Ambiguity Resides in Structures

Ambiguity shows up differently across instruments and layers:

- **Primary Carriers.** Face the front-line effect in claim frequency, severity, and adjustment friction. Ambiguity widens loss picks and raises the cost of capital.

- **Quota Share Reinsurance.** Shares both premium and loss; ambiguity inflates ceding commissions and narrows brokered capacity.

- **Excess-of-Loss (XoL).** Ambiguity primarily distorts the **attachment** (when losses pierce the layer) and the **exhaustion** (how deep they run). Unclear legal dynamics widen the modeled "error bars," lifting rate on line.

- **Industry Loss Warranties (ILWs) & Index Triggers.** Reduce some contract uncertainty but introduce **basis risk**. If legal dynamics inflate indemnity losses without moving industry indices equivalently, sponsors fear protection gaps; investors fear misalignment.

- **Catastrophe Bonds.** Prefer clear, standardized wordings. Ambiguity triggers wider investor due diligence, higher spreads, or refusal to fund.

In short: ambiguity does not merely make deals pricier; it **changes which deals exist at all.**

A Committee Room Vignette: Three Voices, One Decision

Picture a reinsurance committee in London or Zurich.

- **The Chief Risk Officer:** "Modeled expected loss is 3.0% for this Florida book. But variance under legal stress is unbounded. Our back-tests show that when fee dynamics shift, the tail fattens by 30–50% versus cat-only scenarios."

- **The Portfolio Manager:** "If we need an extra 400 bps to compensate for that tail, the cedent won't pay it. If we can't get paid for the uncertainty, the rational allocation is to move capacity to portfolios where the odds are bounded."

- **The Independent Director:** "Our job is not to be brave; it is to be prudent. Hurricanes we accept. Rule instability we decline."

The motion carries: reduce Florida weight or insist on price and terms that are unlikely to clear. Capacity shrinks. That decision will be felt not in a boardroom, but on a renewal notice in Fort Myers.

Quantifying the Unquantifiable: A Practical Heuristic

Because you cannot model ambiguity directly, prudent shops use heuristics:

1. **Uncertainty Premium (UP).** Add a margin to expected loss or to the discount rate proportional to a jurisdiction's rule-change frequency and severity. UP rises non-linearly after shocks.

2. **Participation Caps.** Limit total exposure to jurisdictions with unstable regimes regardless of apparent price.

3. **Trigger Preference.** Favor parametric or index triggers when indemnity exposure is most vulnerable to legal drift, accepting some basis risk to avoid legal ambiguity.

4. **Optionality Clauses.** Insert reset or step-up features when regulatory outcomes are pending, turning unknowns into priced options.

These are engineering responses to a social problem. The better solution is to **reduce the source of ambiguity itself**.

Humor, Because Gravity Needs Levity

If markets could talk during a volatile legislative season, they might say: "We were happily drawing from Jar A—until someone swapped the labels and the **ducks started quacking in a different language**." Or to borrow another image: **the angry bear jumped into the canoe and began rowing us backward**. The humor is not flippancy; it is a shorthand for the real, measurable cost of legal surprises. Every joke here has a price tag on a homeowner's bill.

Turning Jar B into Jar A: Converting Ambiguity into Risk

No one can turn off hurricanes. But leaders can convert ambiguity into risk—turn Jar B into Jar A—by design:

1. **Non-Retroactivity as First Principle.** Apply changes only to policies written after an announced effective date. Yesterday's price cannot fund today's surprise duty.
2. **Advance Notice & Comment.** Release exposure drafts; hold technical hearings; set lead times so underwriters and reinsurers can price the new regime. Process is the antidote to fear.
3. **Plain Language in Statutes and Policies.** Draft coverage, fee, and assignment rules narrowly and clearly; ambiguity in the text becomes severity in the loss.
4. **Operational Realism.** Calibrate claims timelines, documentation, and penalties to catastrophe realities—surge in volume, power outages, supply constraints—so good-faith operations are not criminalized by circumstance.
5. **Fast, Fair Dispute Paths.** Expand appraisal and mediation with bounded timelines to prevent routine disagreements from metastasizing into systemic litigation.
6. **Mitigation as a Market Standard.** Tie material premium credits and public grants to verifiable upgrades (roof decks, openings, garage doors, elevation). Lower expected loss and correlation; reinsurance follows.
7. **Data Transparency.** Require anonymized reporting on claim outcomes, litigation rates, and cycle times so reforms can be tuned empirically. Ambiguity shrinks when facts grow.
8. **Residual Market Guardrails.** Keep the insurer of last resort solvent, fairly priced, and on a credible depopulation path. Capacity believes guardrails more than promises.[14]
9. **Sunset and Review.** Major changes should sunset or be reviewed on schedule; living rules are less frightening than immortal experiments.

These are not "industry favors." They are consumer protection in slow motion: the kind that lowers price by lowering fear.

The Human Angle: Three Vignettes

Maria, Homeowner. She invested in shutters and a strapped roof. She did what every brochure urged her to do. Her premium still jumped. Why? Because she is paying not just for wind, but for the **ambiguity load** others created. Her household balance sheet is the pass-through point for institutional indecision.

Evan, Insurance Agent. He spends renewal season translating jar theory into kitchen-table reality. "Yes, you improved the roof. No, I can't hold last year's price. The reinsurers added an uncertainty premium after the courts shifted the rules." Evan has thick skin; he wishes he had thicker statutes.

Priya, Portfolio Manager. She wants Florida in the portfolio. The yields can be attractive; the peril is diversifying. But her investment committee will not authorize exposure without credible non-retroactivity and signs that litigation incentives are stable. "Bring me Jar A," they tell her, "And we're buyers."

These are not villains and heroes. They are citizens reacting rationally to the signals we send.

A Structured Thought Experiment: Pricing the Unknown

Suppose two otherwise identical portfolios of Florida wind:

- **Portfolio A (Stable Rules).** Expected loss 4.0%. Standard deviation 7.0%. Tail (1-in-100) 25%. Required margin over risk-free for target return: 600 bps.
- **Portfolio B (Rule Drift).** Same modeled peril numbers, but add legal-process variance that fat-tails the distribution: effective standard deviation 9.5%. Tail (1-in-100) 35%. Required margin: 1,000 bps, **if** the sponsor accepts the price—which many cannot.

If the sponsor cannot or will not pay 1,000 bps, capacity shrinks, often invisibly. What appears later as a "sudden premium spike" is frequently last year's capacity decision arriving on the homeowner's desk.

This is not an indictment of sponsors or investors. It is a proof that **ambiguity has a price**, even when no one writes it on the quote.

Policy Pitfalls: When Good Intentions Raise the Ambiguity Toll

- **Blanket Post-Event Relief.** Compassion that alters obligations retroactively invites future scarcity. Targeted grants and mitigation aid do not.

- **Overbroad Drafting.** Words that feel generous today become weapons tomorrow. Precision is kindness to future policyholders.

- **Punitive Timelines.** Post-catastrophe operations cannot be built for blue-sky volumes. Penalty structures that ignore surge dynamics distort behavior and cost.

- **Unbounded Residual Growth.** When last-resort insurers grow without a credible glidepath, private capital prices in the risk that economics will be subordinated to politics.

None of these critique compassion. They critique **delivery mechanisms** that turn mercy into ambiguity.

Practical Metrics: How to Tell if Jar B is Becoming Jar A

Policymakers and market watchers can track an "ambiguity dashboard":

- **Spread Compression.** Are cat bond and XoL spreads tightening relative to modeled loss after reforms?

- **Capacity Mix.** Are new global investors entering, and are sidelined reinsurers returning?

- **Term Improvements.** Are attachment points stabilizing, hours clauses standardizing, and wordings converging?

- **Litigation Ratios.** Are claim-to-suit and suit-to-settlement ratios trending toward catastrophe-only baselines?

- **Depopulation Pace.** Is residual market exposure returning to private balance sheets on a schedule the market believes?

- **Mitigation Uptake.** Are fortified roof credits, opening protections, and garage door reinforcements scaling materially?

These are the footprints of shrinking ambiguity. They appear months before renewal headlines improve.

Rhetorical Gut-Checks (Because Discipline Fades Without Questions)

- If a rule is wise, why must it reach backward to bind contracts priced yesterday?

- If a statute is clear, why do we need courts to supply meaning after every storm?

- If mitigation lowers loss, why does any subsidy dollar go elsewhere before buying down that risk?

- If residual markets grow, who owns the calendar for handing risk back—and what convinces capital to believe it?

Markets answer these questions with spreads and capacity. Homeowners answer them at the kitchen table.

The Ethics of Predictability

There is an ethical dimension to all this. Predictability is not merely an investor preference; it is **justice** for the household that planned in good faith. When we change rules mid-stream, we do not just spook capital; we punish prudence. Families that saved, mitigated, and insured find themselves financing the ambiguity created elsewhere. Reforms that restore predictability restore fairness.

Conversely, when we leave ambiguity in place to avoid hard conversations, the costs migrate—to renters, to first-time buyers, to fixed-income seniors—through higher premiums and reduced availability. The bill always lands somewhere. Predictability makes sure it lands where it can be budgeted, not where it causes the most harm.

Bridges to Finance: Why Pre-Event Capital Beats Post-Event Debt

Ambiguity corrodes **pre-event** capital. Investors demand higher returns or withhold funds. The state then drifts toward **post-event** debt—assessments, bonds, or taxes issued after the disaster. Pre-event capital is equity-like; it absorbs losses without a claim on future taxpayers. Post-event debt is a mortgage on tomorrow. Reducing ambiguity keeps financing on the **front end**, where it is cheaper and fairer.

In that sense, clarity is fiscal conservatism: it pays the bill before the storm, not after, and it pays it with voluntary capital that can leave if mistreated.

A Closing Metaphor: The Carnival Booth

Imagine a carnival booth where you pay to draw a jellybean. The sign says, "Win if you draw red." At the first booth, you can see the jar: 50 red, 50 black. The barker shouts a fair price, and people line up. At the second booth, the jar is covered. The barker promises it's fair—but he also reserves the right to change the rules after you pay. How much would you wager? Most of us smile, shake our heads, and walk on.

Florida's challenge is to be the first booth. Transparent jar. Stable rules. Fair price. No tricks. Capital will play that game all day.

Comparative Snapshot: Two Jurisdictions, Same Storm, Different Outcomes

Consider two coastal regions hit by similar storms within a few seasons of each other. Both suffer heavy wind damage. Both rely on private carriers plus global reinsurance. In Region One, statutes are stable, fee rules are bounded, and a mitigation standard has been in place for years with visible uptake. In Region Two, fee rules oscillate, coverage is litigated into expansion, and reforms are often retroactive.

Twelve months later, Region One's reinsurance renewal is painful but orderly: capacity trims at the margin, spreads widen modestly, and most programs place on schedule. Homeowners see increases that hurt but do not shock. In Region Two, capacity arrives late and conditional, attachments move higher, hours clauses tighten, and several programs require emergency backstops. The average homeowner cannot see the boardroom deliberations that produced this gap. What they feel is the clearing price of ambiguity. The storm was the same; the **rules** were not. In practice, the second region added a second storm—man-made and preventable.

This comparison matters for Florida because capital is global and comparative by nature. Money can buy California quake, European wind, Japanese typhoon, or diversified global ILW baskets. To attract its share, Florida must look more like Region One—not by lucking into fewer hurricanes, but by building a track record of predictability that shows up in the market's own metrics: tighter spreads relative to expected loss, steadier placements, cleaner terms, and returning capacity from counterparties who had stepped back.

A Short FAQ for Skeptics

Q: Isn't capital just using "uncertainty" as an excuse to charge more?

A: Capital chases yield. If ambiguity could be priced cleanly, investors would happily stay and collect the premium. They withdraw not because they dislike profit, but because they cannot define the downside. That is Ellsberg on a term sheet.

Q: Can't we simply cap rates and force participation?

A: You can force a number; you cannot force a balance sheet to remain solvent or a global investor to show up next year. Caps may buy time, but if the underlying ambiguity remains, supply shrinks or flees to places with clearer rules. The bill returns as scarcity, surcharges, or taxes.

Q: Aren't models themselves uncertain?

A: Yes—models are approximations. But their uncertainty is **risk-like**: you can stress, back-test, and diversify it. Legal or policy ambiguity is **uncertainty-like**: it changes the game after the bet is placed. Markets can price noisy weather; they cannot price moving goalposts.

Q: Isn't litigation simply a way to enforce contracts?

A: Properly bounded, yes. But when the incentives around litigation magnify severity far beyond the underlying loss, the contract's economics are rewritten. Predictable, fast dispute paths protect consumers better than a system that turns every disagreement into a tail event.

Implementation Playbook: A 12-Month Agenda to Shrink Ambiguity

If this chapter feels abstract, here is a concrete, time-boxed plan any jurisdiction could execute without waiting for a perfect political moment.

Month 0–2: Diagnose and Signal.

- Convene a technical task force (regulator, carriers, reinsurers, consumer advocates, actuaries).
- Publish a baseline dashboard: claim outcomes, litigation ratios, time-to-payment, reinspection rates, mitigation uptake.
- Announce guiding principles: non-retroactivity, advance notice, operational realism, fast dispute paths, and data transparency.

Month 3–4: Draft with Precision.

- Release exposure drafts for fee rules, assignment mechanics, and dispute processes.
- Use examples in the text ("safe harbors") to reduce interpretive wiggle room.
- Publish proposed effective dates at least six months out to allow pricing.

Month 5–6: Build the Fast Lane.

- Stand up a statewide appraisal/mediation track with certified neutrals, bounded timelines, and standardized forms.
- Create a catastrophe claims protocol that recognizes surge realities (power outages, material shortages) so good-faith failures are not penalized as bad faith.

Month 7–8: Fund Mitigation at Scale.

- Launch grant and low-interest loan programs targeted at roof decks, opening protections, and reinforced garage doors—the three highest-leverage residential upgrades.
- Mandate that carriers file and earn meaningful credits for verified upgrades; publish the credit table so homeowners can plan.

Month 9–10: Guardrail the Residual.

- Adopt a glidepath for depopulation with measurable milestones.

- Require periodic solvency and exposure disclosures understandable to non-experts.
- Prohibit cross-subsidies that encourage persistent underpricing of high-hazard zones.

Month 11–12: Review and Reset.

- Re-publish the dashboard. Where did metrics improve? Where did they stall?
- Tune statutes and protocols based on data, not anecdotes.
- Announce next-year effective dates now; predictability compounds.

This agenda is not glamorous. It is **governance**: the patient work of turning Jar B into Jar A—one clause, one credit, one dashboard at a time.

Bridge to the Next Chapter: Florida's Family Album of Storms

We have established the psychology and the finance of ambiguity. Next, we turn to history—Florida's actual storms and the policy responses that followed them. The question is not whether nature is dangerous; it is whether we compound nature's danger with man-made ambiguity. In the next chapter, we will review the "family album" of hurricanes and trace how different choices either invited capital to stay or taught it to leave.

One-Page Summary (for the busy reader)

- **Ellsberg Paradox** shows that people and markets prefer known odds to unknown odds—**risk** over **uncertainty**.
- In insurance finance, that preference sets price, appetite, and structure. Known hurricane risk can be modeled and funded. Unknown rule shifts cannot.
- Ambiguity enters through **coverage creep, fee dynamics, retroactivity, operational unrealism, and residual market distortion.**
- The result is an invisible **ambiguity load** that raises spreads, shrinks capacity, and lands as higher homeowner premiums and tighter terms.
- Leaders can convert ambiguity into risk with **non-retroactivity, advance notice, plain drafting, operational realism, fast dispute paths, mitigation, data transparency, residual guardrails, and scheduled review.**
- Predictability is not industry charity; it is **consumer protection** and **fiscal prudence**. It pays for losses with pre-event capital instead of post-event debt.
- Florida doesn't need perfect weather to keep capital. It needs a jar with visible beans and rules that don't change after you've paid to play.

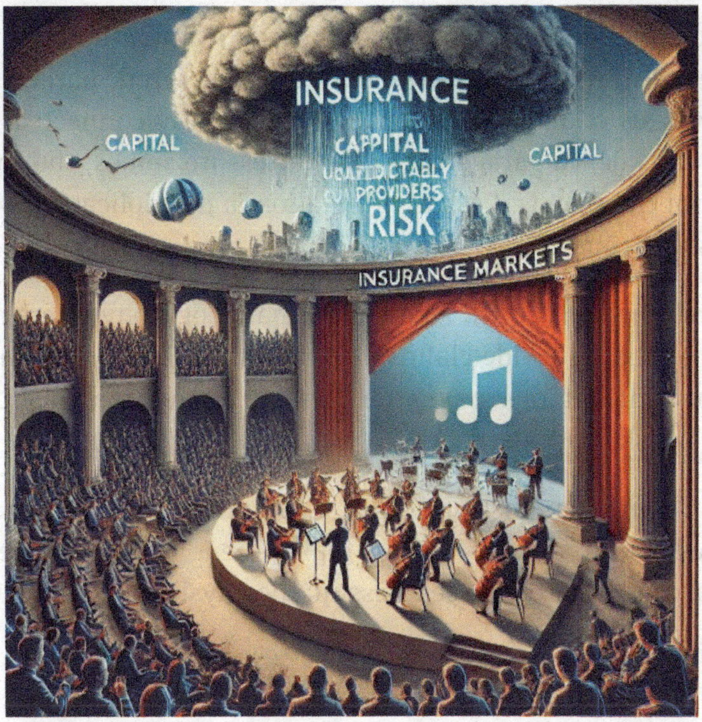

Chapter 4 – Florida: The Perfect Storm of Policy and Hurricanes

What breaks a market faster—catastrophe winds or a crisis of confidence? In Florida, the answer has too often been "both at the same time." Nature brings the wind; we supply the whiplash. The result is a **perfect storm** in the strictest sense: physical peril colliding with policy improvisation, producing losses that no actuarial table can tame and no homeowner can budget for. This chapter is Florida's story—part weather report, part case study in incentives—told with one purpose: to show how predictable rules can make even a hurricane-soaked state insurable, and how unpredictable rules can make even calm seasons unaffordable.

The Family Album of Storms: What Nature Teaches (When We Listen)

Open Florida's family album and you meet recurring characters—Andrew, Charley, Ivan, Jeanne, Wilma, Irma, Michael, Ian—each leaving a fingerprint on building practices, pricing, and the availability of capital.

- **Andrew (1992):** The market's rude awakening. Andrew did not merely destroy homes; it revealed weak construction practices and fragile capitalization. In Andrew's aftermath, Florida strengthened codes, rethought solvency, and institutionalized pre-event risk spreading (most notably through statewide reinsurance backstops). **Lesson:** hardening standards and clear financing mechanisms pull the market back from the brink.

- **The 2004–2005 Gauntlet (Charley, Frances, Ivan, Jeanne; then Wilma):** A stress test for everything we learned from Andrew. Some counties fared markedly better where code enforcement was strict and roof systems were properly connected. Others showed how **small failures cascade**—a garage door gives, pressure spikes, the roof lifts, and interior becomes exterior in seconds. **Lesson:** mitigation is multiplicative. One weak component can erase five strong ones.

- **Irma (2017) and Michael (2018):** A reminder that geography offers no immunity. Irma's long footprint tested statewide claims operations; Michael's compact ferocity punished any illusion that only big metros matter. **Lesson:** operations must be catastrophe-scale realistic, not blue-sky optimized.

- **Ian (2022):** A modern demonstration that **exposure has outpaced memory**. Even where codes improved, sheer density, rising replacement costs, and legacy vulnerabilities combined to produce outsized losses. **Lesson:** the physics of wind met the mathematics of growth—and growth won.

Nature's part in the story is not mysterious. Hurricanes will strike with uneven rhythm. Losses will be heavy in some years, light in others. This is **risk**—violent, yes, but measurable over time. What we do with that risk—how we build, insure, litigate, finance, and govern—decides whether capital stays or leaves.

Florida Chronology: Storms & Policy Pivots (2004–2023) — See Appendix A[15]

Florida's timeline shows a repeating pattern: storm seasons test roofs, and the season after tests rules. Appendix A aligns landfalls with legal and operational pivots. When changes are **prospective** and **plain-language**, we see spreads compress over the next placement; when changes are **retroactive** or incentive-distorting, spreads widen—even without a major storm.

Spectrum check: Prospectivity moves the dot left; retroactivity shoves it right.

Exposure Outran Wisdom: The Growth–Risk Trap

Florida's population and **Total Insured Value (TIV)** have grown faster than our collective appetite for blunt truth. When homes and businesses multiply in wind-exposed zones faster than mitigation and infrastructure upgrade, the system accumulates **correlated risk**—many structures subject to the same hazard profile at the same time. The **Law of Large Numbers** still holds, but correlated losses make the law work more slowly and expensively.

Two implications matter:

1. **Price is a compass, not a punishment.** If a coastal ZIP code faces higher expected losses, premiums must signal that reality or builders and buyers will continue to cluster in the red. Muffle the signal, and you do not eliminate risk—you subsidize its growth.
2. **Mitigation pays twice.** It reduces expected loss **and** reduces correlation—thinning the tail of the distribution that reinsurers price most dearly. A sealed roof deck, strapped trusses, reinforced garage doors, and protected openings do not merely lower average losses; they reduce the chance that an entire neighborhood fails at once.

There is no honest path to affordability that bypasses these two facts.

Codes, Enforcement, and the "One Weak Link" Problem

After Andrew, Florida moved toward a unified, modern **Florida Building Code**. Where enforcement is consistent and reroofing/retrofitting requirements are real (not just ink on paper), claims severity falls—often dramatically. But codes live in the world of **margins**: a few millimeters of nail embedment, the distance between ring-shank and smooth shank, the continuity of a load path, the quality of a garage door track. In catastrophe, tiny engineering details are the difference between "messy but intact" and "slab only." That's why **standard** + **enforcement** + **inspection** is a three-legged stool; remove any leg, and the promise wobbles.[16]

Two practical truths:

- **Reroof moments are golden.** Most homes will be re-roofed once or twice over a mortgage life. If those touchpoints require sealed decks, secondary water barriers, and proper fastening, the state quietly upgrades millions of roofs without a single ribbon-cutting. The cheapest mitigation is the mitigation piggy-backed on something the homeowner was going to do anyway.
- **Credits must be credible.** When premium credits for mitigation are meaningful and predictable—and when verification is friction-light and trusted—contractors have a business reason to sell upgrades and homeowners have a financial reason to buy them. If the credit is token or unreliable, uptake stalls.

A code on paper is law. A code in price is culture.

Claims Reality at Cat Scale: Operations vs. Wishful Thinking

Everyone loves "fast and fair." But after a major landfall, volume, power loss, supply chain snarls, and labor constraints collide. A claims process calibrated to a normal week will **fail at scale**. When laws treat scale failure as malice, uncertainty rises. The fix is not to lower expectations; it is to **design for surge**:

- Pre-approved, standardized **temporary repairs** protocols that stop secondary damage without turning every tarp into a litigation trigger.
- Realistic, catastrophe-aware **timelines** for inspections, documentation, and payments—with explicit safe harbors when external constraints (no materials, no power, no access) make deadlines physically impossible.
- Expanded, bounded **appraisal/mediation** channels to resolve disputes quickly, before friction becomes severity.

Well-designed operations shrink uncertainty by signaling: "Here is what you can expect from us; here is what we expect from you; and here is the clock both of us must live by when the grid is down."

Litigation Incentives: When Friction Becomes Severity

Florida is not unique in having disputes after storms. But the **incentive structure**—how fees are awarded, how assignments of benefits work, how penalties attach—can transform everyday friction into systemic severity. Insurers price **expected loss** from wind and water; they cannot price **open-ended legal multipliers** that materialize after bills are due. The result is a quiet surcharge that never appears as a line item: an **ambiguity load** embedded in reinsurance, capital costs, and ultimately in homeowner premiums.

The point is not to attack anyone's right to redress. The point is to **bound it**. When rules clearly define obligations, timelines, and remedies, most disagreements resolve on their merits; when rules are vague or retroactive, the path of least resistance is a lawsuit. Markets respond by charging for the fog.[17]

Residual Markets: Lifeline or Long-Term Detour?

Every catastrophe-exposed jurisdiction needs a safety valve—an **insurer of last resort** that catches those whom private markets cannot (for a time) cover. The trouble begins when the lifeline becomes the default lane. If residual market growth feels unbounded or politically insulated from risk-based price signals, private carriers read the message: **we will be undercut when we are prudent and blamed when we are not.** Capacity shrinks or leaves. Conversely, a transparent glidepath back to private markets, backed by credible depopulation milestones, is a powerful signal that discipline—not headlines—drives design.

A residual market is a tool. Whether it becomes a bridge back to private capacity—or a bypass around it—depends on governance, price adequacy, and the credible promise that today's emergency is not tomorrow's entitlement.

The Hard Market Mechanism: How Capacity Leaves (and Returns)

It is useful to demystify capital's behavior. Markets are not moody; they are comparative. Investors can deploy to Florida wind, California quake, European windstorm, Japanese typhoon, or diversified industry-loss instruments. They scan for two things: **yield** and **rule stability**. If Florida's yield adjusted for **ambiguity** looks inferior to alternatives, capacity steps back. Often you don't see the decision until renewal, when placements get harder, terms tighten, and attachments drift upward.

Capacity returns the same way it left—by comparison. When jurisdictional rules signal crisp non-retroactivity, operational realism, and clear dispute paths; when mitigation uptake is measurable and credits are real; when residual market governance announces and meets depopulation milestones—spreads tighten relative to modeled loss, and sidelined players resume writing. The market has only two speeds: **fear** and **trust**. Statutes and enforcement decide the gear.

Deeper Dive: Quantifying Capital Flight Patterns (see Appendix E)

Track the same signals every renewal: carrier **exits**, reinsurance **rate-on-line** shifts, **attachment** creep, **trapped collateral**, and the **litigation share** of losses. Appendix E flags an instructive episode where a rate freeze opened a double-digit gap and was followed by exits within 18 months. The peril was constant; the **process** changed. Treat these as early warnings, not post-mortems.

Spectrum check: When warning lights flash, capital prices process, not peril.

Florida as Case Study: Two Storms, One Market

Consider a composite vignette drawn from actual patterns:

- **Before the storm:** Builders and buyers continue to favor water-proximate parcels. Codes exist and are generally strong, but enforcement is uneven and reroof triggers are variably applied. Premiums have been held below risk-adequate levels for years, with political pressure to "smooth" increases. A handful of carriers have thin capital cushions; reinsurance terms have tightened.
- **After landfall:** Claims surge, materials are scarce, adjusters and contractors are over-subscribed. Emergency measures are announced—some prudent, some retroactive. Disputes escalate; fee incentives spur volume over resolution. Residual market policies jump as non-renewals ripple through subsequent seasons.
- **At reinsurance:** Committees widen "error bars" on expected loss—not for wind, but for **process**. Those who stay demand higher rates on line; those who leave shift to jurisdictions where law behaves predictably even when weather does not.

- **On Main Street:** Homeowners with mitigation still see sharp increases because they are paying for process risk they did not create. Agents explain; consumers fume; legislators promise action.

This loop is not fate. It is design. Break the chain at any link—credible non-retroactivity, operational realism, real mitigation credits, transparent depopulation—and the loop loosens. Break several links and the loop opens. Capital notices.

Data Without the Drama: What to Track (So Policy Isn't Guesswork)

Markets respond to metrics. Florida can anchor decisions in a simple public **dashboard**:

1. Citizens/Residual Market Share: Absolute policies, share of statewide risk, and depopulation velocity.
2. Mitigation Uptake: Share of homes with verified sealed decks, strapped trusses, reinforced garage doors, and opening protections; average premium credit by feature.
3. Claims Cycle Times: Reported to payment; disputed to resolution; catastrophe vs. non-cat baselines; variance by county.
4. Litigation Ratios: Claims-to-suit, suit-to-settlement, average fee ratios; trends pre- and post-reform.
5. Reinsurance Terms vs. Modeled Loss: Attachment points, rate on line, and hours clauses relative to peril expectations.
6. Non-Retroactivity Score: A count of meaningful rule changes and whether they were prospective or retroactive.

When this dashboard improves, capacity returns **before** consumers see relief. When it worsens, capacity leaves **before** consumers feel pain. The lag hides the cause; the dashboard unmasks it.

What Worked (So We Can Scale It)

Florida has piloted solutions that deserve scaling:

- **Code Modernization + Enforcement:** Counties with strict inspection and consistent application of reroof triggers see fewer severe claims. The ROI is quiet but compounding.
- **Targeted Mitigation Grants and Loans:** Programs that subsidize the highest-leverage upgrades (roof deck sealing, opening protection, garage door reinforcement) move households from "at risk" to "resilient" for a fraction of post-event aid.
- **Credible Premium Credits:** When carriers must file and honor material credits for verified mitigation, contractors sell upgrades and homeowners buy them.

- **Pre-Event Financing:** Reinsurance and capital market participation purchased **before** the storm is almost always cheaper than debt placed **after** the storm. Pre-funding turns taxpayers into customers rather than guarantors.

None of these depend on the weather. All of them depend on the will to institutionalize what works.

What Failed (So We Can Stop Doing It)

- **Rate Suppression:** Holding prices below risk for political comfort compounds exposure and drives capacity away. The bill returns as scarcity and volatility.

- **Retroactive "Mercy":** Changing obligations after policies are bound feels compassionate and plays well in headlines; it raises the ambiguity load for years.

- **Unrealistic Operational Rules:** Timelines, documentation, and penalty structures that collapse at catastrophe scale turn good-faith work into legal exposure.

- **Letting Residual Markets Become Permanent:** If last-resort coverage becomes the cheapest or easiest option, private capacity cannot compete on prudence—and exits.

Florida can choose differently. Predictability is not austerity; it is stewardship.

Lessons in Trust (From Version A)

Trust takes seasons to build and one surprise to break. Florida earns durable capacity with boring discipline: **prospective** notice, **narrow** drafting, **cat-realistic** operations, and **bounded** dispute paths. That's not leniency; it's how you buy affordability that lasts.

Spectrum check: Predictability discounts price; surprise surcharges it.

Translating Principle into Policy: A Florida Playbook

This is not a wish list. It is a **do-able** 12–18 month playbook tailored to Florida's lived dynamics:

1. Carve Non-Retroactivity in Stone. Enact and enforce a general non-retroactivity rule for insurance obligations. Prospectivity becomes the default, exceptions require supermajority votes and explicit funding.

2. Publish a Cat-Realistic Claims Protocol. Set timelines and documentation that reflect surge realities; define safe harbors; require clear communication templates to homeowners; train and certify catastrophe-season mediators and appraisers.

3. Make Reroof a Mitigation Moment. Require sealed decks and proper fasteners as part of any permitted reroof statewide; tie meaningful premium credits to verified completion; publish a credit table homeowners can understand.

4. Fund the Three Big Upgrades. Create standing grant/loan programs for sealed decks, opening protection, and reinforced garage doors. Make the application process friction-light; allow contractor-verified completion with random audits.

5. Turn Credits into Culture. Require carriers to file mitigation credits at levels that reflect loss reduction; audit actual application; penalize bad actors. When credits are real, contractors become ambassadors for resilience.

6. Glidepath the Residual Market. Announce yearly depopulation targets; create incentives for private carriers to assume blocks of business; align residual pricing with risk so it is a lifeline, not a magnet.

7. Data Everywhere. Mandate anonymized, quarterly disclosure of claim counts, cycle times, dispute rates, fee ratios, and mitigation uptake. Let the public and capital markets see the same scorecard regulators see.

8. Invite Capital with Contract Certainty. Standardize policy wordings statewide where feasible; promote arbitration/appraisal frameworks with bounded timelines; reduce ambiguity that turns word choice into tail risk.

9. Pre-Event Capital First. Expand participation in global reinsurance and cat bond markets with transparent, rules-based procurement. Use pre-funded capital to reduce reliance on post-event assessments.

10. Sunset & Review. Every major rule change sunsets or faces scheduled review with data-driven hearings. Stability is not "never change"; it is no surprises and measurable outcomes.

This playbook is not partisan. It is actuarial. It treats premium as a signal, mitigation as a strategy, and predictability as consumer protection.

The Human Ledger: Maria's Street After Ian

Walk Maria's Street a year after a major storm. Half the blue tarps are gone; aluminum crews finally got the last stack of garage doors; a few homes sit empty, their owners priced out by a renewal they never saw coming. Two doors down, a retired couple shows off steel panels they bought with a small grant and a contractor discount. Their premium dropped—not to where it was, but enough to breathe.

No one on this street talks about "ambiguity loads" or "rate on line." They talk about **fairness** and **foreseeability**. "If you're going to change the rules," Maria says, "tell me **before** I write the check." That sentence is the entire chapter in ten words. It is also the ethic behind a healthy market: respect the household that plans in good faith.

Humor, because gravity needs levity

I once joked that Florida policy can feel like attending a symphony where the conductor announces mid-movement, "We're switching to jazz." Some audience members love it; investors head for the exit to find Beethoven across town. Or, to borrow another image, everything is going fine **until the ducks start quacking in a different language**—right about the time a post-event rule change arrives. The point of the joke is not cynicism. It is design. If you want capacity to stay for the whole performance, don't change the score after tickets are sold.

Ethics and Economics: The Courage to Be Predictable

Predictability is not a gift to carriers; it is justice for consumers. It honors homeowners who mitigated, paid, and planned. It tells investors the jar of jellybeans has visible contents (known odds), not a cloth over the top. It lets contractors hire and train with confidence. It signals to mayors and councils that growth plans must align with hazard. In short, it turns **risk** back into something insurance is meant to handle—and pushes **uncertainty** out of the kitchen where homeowners do their math.

It also aligns with fiscal conservatism: pre-event capital beats post-event debt, and targeted mitigation beats perpetual subsidy. A predictable market lets public dollars do the most good for the most vulnerable without dissolving incentives for everyone else.

A Short FAQ for Florida Skeptics

Question: "Isn't all of this just code for higher rates?"

Answer: No. It is code for **right rates**—rates that reflect hazard and shrink as mitigation spreads and ambiguity recedes. The only honest route to lower, durable premiums is to lower **expected loss** and **uncertainty**. Everything else is a detour.

Question: "Won't strong non-retroactivity tie our hands in a crisis?"

Answer: It will tie our hands from making **tomorrow's** buyers pay for **yesterday's** decisions. We can still fund relief prospectively—with transparent appropriations, targeted grants, and bridge programs—without charging the whole system with fear.

Question: "Can't we just force carriers to write and cap their prices?"

Answer: You can command a number; you cannot command solvency or global participation. Forced supply is a short road to emptier shelves.

Question: "Does mitigation really move the needle?"

Answer: Yes—when it is the right mitigation, verified, credited, and scaled. The cheapest loss is the one that never happens.

The Bridge to What Comes Next

Chapters 1–3 laid the intellectual scaffolding: the long history of risk, Knight's line between risk and uncertainty, and Ellsberg's psychology of ambiguity. This chapter set those ideas in Florida concrete—literally, in rebar and roof decks—and in Florida statute—figuratively, in rules and incentives. The next step is to translate this design into **finance** and **governance** tools that keep capital present: cleaner contracts, smarter pooling, parametric complements, better bonding between public programs and private capacity, and a depopulation path that the market believes.

The weather will not cooperate. It doesn't have to. If Florida chooses predictability with as much enthusiasm as it chooses sunshine, the perfect storm becomes a manageable season—and **The Capital Drain** becomes, at last, a capital return.

Chapter 5 – The Price of Policy Uncertainty

What, precisely, are we paying for when our premiums jump? The wind? Yes. The shingles? Yes. But more and more, we are paying for **policy uncertainty**—the invisible surcharge that shows up when statutes wobble, court doctrines sprawl, and operational rules are written for blue-sky days rather than storm seasons. Hurricanes break roofs; **uncertainty breaks markets**. And when markets break, the bill migrates to homeowners, taxpayers, and the broader economy.

The Invisible Surcharge

Insurers itemize their costs internally, even if the renewal notice doesn't spell them out. Think of a homeowner's premium as five stacked layers:

1. **Expected Loss (Hazard):** Modeled wind/surge damage over time.
2. **Expense Load:** Distribution, claims staff, IT, compliance.
3. **Risk Load (Capital Cost):** What investors require to stand behind volatility.
4. **Reinsurance/Capital Transfer:** The cost to move tail risk to global markets.
5. **Ambiguity Load (Uncertainty):** The extra return capital demands when **rules**—not weather—are unpredictable.

When policymakers ask, *"Why did rates spike? We didn't change the weather,"* the answer often sits in layer five. Legal and regulatory ambiguity widens tails, erodes model confidence, and makes every other layer more expensive. That is the price of policy uncertainty.

Transmission Mechanisms: How Uncertainty Turns into Dollars

Uncertainty doesn't float in from the Gulf. It arrives through human choices:

- **Coverage Creep:** After big loss years, ambiguous clauses are read to mean more than underwriters priced. A contract written for **X** quietly becomes **X+Y**.
- **Litigation Incentives:** One-way fee structures, multiplier doctrines, and assignment mechanics can transform friction into severity. Routine disagreements become systemic tail events.
- **Retroactivity:** Rule changes that reach backward convert yesterday's priced risk into today's unpriced liability.
- **Operational Unrealism:** Timelines or documentation rules that collapse at catastrophe scale automatically criminalize good-faith claims handling.

- **Residual Market Distortion**: When the plan of last resort becomes the **largest** plan—without a credible glide path back—private capital infers that economics will be subordinated to politics.

Each is a pipeline that carries uncertainty straight into price.

When the Same Wind Costs More

The hurricane didn't change. The county did. Last year, under a modern code and a quiet rulebook, a carrier priced a block of homes at the **Judgmental Risk** zone—messy but manageable. Then, a late-session change expanded fee exposure in disputes that used to resolve in appraisal. A court, citing fresh language, read a coverage clause more broadly than any prior filing assumed. Overnight, nothing about the wind was different. Everything about the **process** was.

Inside the carrier, the loss pick didn't explode. The *error bars* did. Inside the reinsurance shop, the debate shifted from "What's our AAL?" to "What on earth is our tail now?" Committees don't shout; they slide dots. The portfolio that lived left of center now sits in **Regime-Sensitive Risk**. When you see the world this way, you understand why the reinsurance quote came back higher, why the attachment crept up, why the broker cleared capacity later than usual. And, eventually, why Maria's renewal ticked up even though she bought shutters. She paid not for wind, but for a nudge **right** on the spectrum delivered by people who will never see her kitchen table.

There is a moral in this arithmetic: households should not pay for surprises they did not create. The only way to honor that is to write a rulebook that does not surprise. The wind will do enough of that for all of us.

Premiums vs. Exposure: When the Compass Spins

Price is not punishment; price is a **compass**. It points at hazard, construction quality, and process risk. When we muffle or misdirect that compass—via temporary suppressions or policy improvisations—we don't make risk cheaper; we **displace** it. Builders and buyers keep clustering in red zones because the signal is soft. Losses grow. Reinsurance responds. Rate relief passed today becomes rate shock tomorrow.

Yes, there are households who cannot carry the load that a truthful compass displays. The answer is not to break the compass; it is to **pair** risk-based pricing with **targeted** help (grants, credits, loans) and with measurable **mitigation** that lowers loss for everyone.

The Reinsurance Echo

Reinsurance is Florida's shock absorber, but it echoes back whatever we put into it. If we send the market a clear, prospective rulebook, reinsurers will quote capacity at spreads tied to modeled peril. If we send ambiguity, they will quote **fear** or decline entirely. A single late-session legal change can cost homeowners far more than any one storm because it reprices entire portfolios—not just the damaged homes, but all the *could-be* homes embedded in every return-period curve.

Reinsurers are not moody. They are comparative. They can fund Florida wind, European windstorm, Japanese typhoon—whatever offers the best ratio of yield to **rule stability**. If we want the world's balance sheets in our corner, we must make Florida's rules look like a **straight line**, not a seismograph.

One Renewal Season, Week by Week

Week 1 — The model prints stable hazard, but quotes arrive wider than last year. The table talk isn't wind; it's wordings. A senior underwriter asks three times whether post-event fee dynamics are truly bounded this season. No one mentions a forecast.

Week 2 — Attachment points edge up. Not because the roofs changed, but because tails feel fatter when dispute paths look unbounded. A cat bond desk that was keen in March now wants an extra quarter-point and tighter hours clauses.

Week 3 — Two panel names decline to renew entirely. The tender doesn't fail, but it shrinks. The placement still clears—higher—but you can feel the bid/ask spread widen with each ambiguous answer.

Week 4 — A small change lands: a plain, prospective notice on appraisal timelines and a posted claims protocol for grid-down conditions. Spreads don't collapse, but they stop widening. One desk increases its line. Nothing meteorological happened. The rulebook did.

That is how price tells you what the models cannot. When investors can see and trust the path the words will take after landfall, capital leans in. When they cannot, the season becomes defense, and defense is expensive.

Spectrum check: Clarity trims the spread every week it's posted; ambiguity widens it before the wind ever blows.

Citizens and the Crowd-Out Risk

A residual market is a vital **lifeline**—not a permanent lane. When Citizens (or any last-resort plan) grows large and sticky, it changes incentives. Private carriers read the signal: prudence will be undercut by subsidized alternatives when politics gets hot. Investors read it too: losses may migrate to future assessments or taxes, but in the meantime, private balance sheets can't price against a moving target.

The cure is governance by **guardrail**: Risk-adequate, transparent pricing; a published depopulation glidepath; and credible milestones that capital believes. When the lifeline becomes a bridge **back** to private markets, capacity follows. When it becomes a bypass **around** them, capacity leaves.

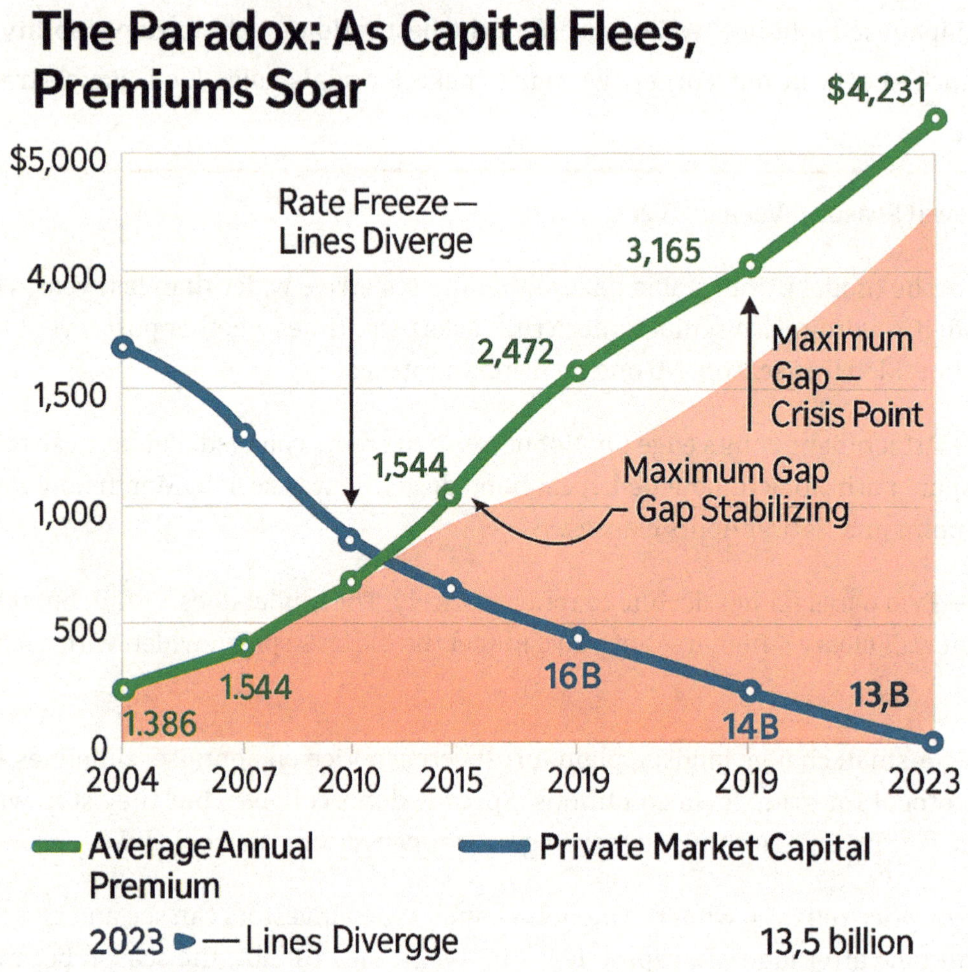

Figure 5.1- The uncertainty tax: as private market capital falls, average premiums rise. Lines diverge after policy interventions that increase adjudication/operational ambiguity; they begin to converge only when rules become prospective and plain-language. See Appendix E (Indicators) and Appendix H (data series).

Let's be candid: litigation enforces contracts. But incentives matter. If counsel is rewarded for prolonging disputes rather than solving them, the system inflates losses beyond hazard. That does not help Maria (our homeowner) get her roof replaced faster. It increases what her next-door neighbor pays at renewal.

Bounded, predictable **dispute paths**—appraisal, mediation, arbitration with firm timelines—de-escalate conflict. They honor consumer rights **and** protect the pool from tail risks that have nothing to do with wind speed.

"Rabbit Chase, Chicken Chase": A Florida Parable

I once told a story in about **rabbit chases** and **chicken chases**—a light jab at policymaking by adrenaline. We sprint after the rabbit we see (today's angry headline), while the fox (tomorrow's capital flight) strolls off with the henhouse. Or we chase chickens around the yard, proud of our cardio, while the fence lies open.

It's funny because it's true. Post-event improvisation can feel like action. But if the action injects uncertainty—retroactive changes, fuzzy wordings, unrealistic timelines—it teaches capital one lesson: "This yard is chaotic." The joke lands; the bill lands harder.

The Economic Spillovers: Not Just an Insurance Story

The price of uncertainty doesn't stop at the policy. It seeps into:

- **Housing Affordability:** A thousand-dollar jump in wind premium can erase a mortgage pre-approval. Demand softens; local wealth tied to home equity deflates.
- **Local Credit Markets:** Regional banks and credit unions rely on insurable collateral. Unstable insurance terms can stall lending or push borrowers into riskier products.
- **Municipal Budgets:** Rising premiums for public buildings and infrastructure crowd out core services; post-event debt service grows when pre-event capital avoids the jurisdiction.
- **Small Business Balance Sheets:** Restaurants, contractors, and medical practices face rising commercial premiums and business interruption uncertainties; some delay expansion, some exit.

Labor Markets: Workers priced out of coastal rents move inland or out-of-state; employers face higher wage floors to offset living costs.

If we pretend this is an "industry" issue, we miss the systemic risk. The state's growth engine relies on insurable roofs and predictable rules.

Case Vignettes: The Price, Up Close

Maria, Fort Myers: She strapped the roof, added shutters, and bought a reinforced garage door. She "did the brochure." Her premium still jumped. Why? Because the **ambiguity load** rose after a post-storm legal change. Maria paid for a rule she didn't write.

Evan, Insurance Agent: He spends evenings explaining why mitigation helped—but not enough to outrun the reinsurance echo. His desk is where market theory meets human frustration. He needs statutes that make his explanations shorter.

Priya, Portfolio Manager: She wants Florida in the fund. The peril diversifies her book. But her investment committee will not authorize exposure unless they can **see the jar** (Ellsberg): non-retroactivity, bounded fee rules, and a credible Citizens glidepath. She's not being difficult; she's doing her job.

Operations at Scale: Designing for Surge, Not for Slogans

Fast-and-fair isn't a bumper sticker. It's a **design problem**. After landfall, power is out, roads are blocked, materials scarce, adjusters oversubscribed. If rules assume normal volume and full supply chains, they criminalize good-faith performance. Then dispute becomes default.

A better pattern:

- **Cat-Aware Timelines:** Deadlines that flex with declared states of emergency and objectively measured constraints.
- **Standardized Temporary Repairs:** Pre-approved scope and rates reduce suspicion and speed stabilization.
- **Bounded Dispute Channels:** Appraisal or mediation with strict clocks and limited fee exposure lowers systemic severity.

This is consumer protection in the language capital understands.

Mitigation: The Only Honest Shortcut to Affordability

Mitigation is **price control without politics**. Strapped trusses, sealed decks, opening protection, and reinforced garage doors reduce **expected loss** and **correlation**. Lower correlation thins the tail that reinsurance prices most dearly. That math drops straight to the renewal. It's not a slogan; it's a spreadsheet.

Make mitigation unavoidable at natural touchpoints—**reroof** permits, major renovations—and make credits **meaningful**, **verifiable**, and **portable**. Pair that with grants or low-interest loans for vulnerable households. Everyone wins: households, carriers, reinsurers, and—most of all—taxpayers who won't be asked to socialize avoidable losses.

A Model of the Price: Stylized but Useful

Imagine two otherwise identical counties:

County A (Stable Rules): Expected loss 4%, reinsurance rate-on-line reflects hazard. Market clears with standard terms.

County B (Unstable Rules): Same hazard. But fee incentives and retroactivity add process variance. Reinsurers widen error bars, raise prices, and tighten wordings. Some step back entirely.

Homeowners in B pay for **process**, not just peril. Many never learn why their neighbor in A, across a state line or under a different regime, pays less. The answer isn't weather. It's **policy**.

Deeper Dive: Indicators to Watch (Are We Pricing Process—or Peril?)

If you want an early read on whether uncertainty—not wind—is driving price, watch five signals over time, not one season at a time. First, **rate-on-line** versus modeled hazard; when spreads widen faster than peril, process is in the price. Second, **attachment drift**; higher starting points tell you tails feel fatter. Third, **trapped collateral** that lingers into the next renewal; frozen cash is the cost of ambiguity. Fourth, the **litigation share** of losses; when a larger fraction flows through dispute channels, severity multiplies. Fifth, **panel participation** and tender outcomes; failed placements and smaller lines are ballots cast against predictability. Track these together and you won't need a headline to tell you where the dot sits on the Spectrum. Appendix E shows a simple dashboard you can adapt.

Spectrum check: When these lights flash, capital prices the rulebook more than the wind—and households pay the difference.

"Why Can't We Just Cap Rates?"

Because you cannot cap **physics** and you cannot cap **fear**. You can post a number, but you cannot make global capital accept it. Caps without underlying stability shrink supply and push risk back onto residual markets or taxpayers. The short-term applause is loud; the long-term bill is larger.

If the goal is lower, durable prices, there are only two levers that move the needle: **lower expected loss** (mitigation, codes, siting) and **lower uncertainty** (non-retroactivity, clarity, cat-realistic operations, bounded disputes). Everything else rearranges deck chairs.

Rhetorical Gut-Checks (to keep our discipline)

- If a rule is good, why must it reach backward?
- If a statute is clear, why is every hurricane followed by a wave of interpretive litigation?
- If mitigation pays, why isn't every public dollar before landfall spoken for?
- If Citizens grows, where is the calendar—and what convinces capital it's real?

Markets answer these with spreads and capacity. Households answer them with budgets and moving vans.

A Florida Playbook to Lower the Price of Uncertainty

1. **Carve Non-Retroactivity into Stone.** Prospectivity is the default; exceptions require supermajority votes **and** explicit appropriations.
2. **Publish a Cat-Realistic Claims Protocol.** Timelines, documentation, and safe harbors calibrated to surge realities; standardized temporary repair scopes.
3. **Make Reroof the Big Upgrade.** Require sealed decks/fasteners at reroof; tie meaningful, audited credits to verified completion.
4. **Fast, Fair Dispute Lanes.** Expand appraisal/mediation with hard clocks; cap fee exposure in those lanes to prevent escalation as strategy.
5. **Mitigation Grants/Loans at Scale.** Fund the three highest-leverage upgrades; automate verification; show households the credit table up front.
6. **Citizens Guardrails.** Risk-adequate pricing, transparent solvency metrics, and a public depopulation glidepath with milestones.
7. **Data Dashboard.** Quarterly, anonymized reporting of claim cycle times, litigation ratios, mitigation uptake, reinsurance terms vs. modeled loss.
8. **Standardized Wordings.** Encourage statewide forms where feasible; contract certainty is capital's love language.
9. **Pre-Event Capital First.** Expand reinsurance and cat-bond participation with transparent procurement; front-load finance, avoid post-event debt.
10. **Sunset & Review.** Every major change sunsets or faces scheduled review with data in hand. Stability is **no surprises**, not **never change**.

This is not an industry wish list. It is a consumer-protection agenda that lowers price by lowering fear.

Humor, because gravity needs levity

A friend once said our policy debates feel like playing poker with the cards face up—until someone turns out the lights and insists, we keep betting. That's uncertainty. Or, as your own line puts it, everything is fine **until the ducks start quacking in a different language**. We can laugh, but let's not miss the point: the joke is expensive. It shows up as capacity that doesn't show up.

Ethics: The Justice of Predictability

Predictability honors the prudent. It keeps faith with families who saved, mitigated, paid premiums, and expected fair dealing under a stable rulebook. It protects the vulnerable by channeling aid **before** landfall, not after, and by transforming subsidy into resilience rather than into repeat loss. It tells the truth in price and then helps people respond to that truth.

That is conservatism in practice: pay the bill up front, in full view, with voluntary capital that can leave if mistreated—and treat it so well that it stays.

One-Page Summary

The biggest driver of today's premium pain isn't just wind; it's the **ambiguity load** created by legal and policy unpredictability.

Uncertainty transmits via coverage creep, fee incentives, retroactivity, unrealistic operations, and residual market distortion.

Reinsurance echoes whatever we send it: clarity earns capacity at peril-linked spreads; ambiguity earns fear or exits.

Affordability that lasts comes from two levers: **lower expected loss** (mitigation, codes, siting) and **lower uncertainty** (non-retroactivity, clarity, cat-aware operations, bounded disputes).

A Florida playbook—non-retroactivity, cat-realistic claims, reroof upgrades, fast dispute lanes, mitigation finance, Citizens guardrails, data transparency, standardized wordings, pre-event capital, sunset/review—converts uncertainty back into priceable risk.

Predictability is not an industry favor; it is consumer justice and fiscal prudence.

Bridge to Chapter 6

We've tallied the bill for uncertainty. Next, we'll flip the ledger to the capital side: **how global investors actually size, price, and allocate catastrophe risk**—and what Florida must look like to be a first-call destination for that capital rather than a last-resort solicitation. In short, Chapter 6 will show you how to turn **The Capital Drain** into a **capital return.**

Chapter 6 – When Capital Flees: The Global Investment View

What does it take for the world's balance sheets to underwrite a storm-soaked peninsula year after year? A hurricane can rip off roofs in hours; capital can vanish in minutes. The blunt truth is that Florida isn't competing against the weather—it's competing against every other place on earth where investors can put a dollar to work with clearer rules and steadier odds. Hurricanes are not the villain here. **Ambiguity is.** This chapter looks at Florida through the eyes of those who actually decide whether to commit billions to wind risk: reinsurers, ILS funds, pension trustees, ratings analysts, and Lloyd's syndicates. Their message is consistent: **give us risk, not uncertainty, and we will fund you at scale.**

1) Who "capital" actually is (and what each player wants)

"Capital" is not a single temperament. It's a cast of characters with different time horizons, incentives, and risk tolerances:

- **Traditional reinsurers** (Bermuda, Europe, Lloyd's syndicates): seek multi-year relationships and underwriting margin; recycle risk globally; sensitive to legal drift and loss creep.
- **Collateralized re and ILS funds**: invest through fully collateralized contracts and catastrophe bonds; performance is "mark-to-model" until it isn't; extremely allergic to post-event surprises that **trap collateral**.
- **Pensions and endowments**: like catastrophe exposure because it diversifies equity and credit cycles; require boring, repeatable rules; they don't need drama to hit 7% actuarial targets.
- **Retrocession providers** (reinsurance for reinsurers): price the tail; first to step back when uncertainty fattens that tail beyond model boundaries.
- **Specialty MGAs/fronting carriers**: write to capacity that sits behind them; if that capacity cools, they must shrink, no matter how clever their underwriting is.

Each of these players asks three questions: What is my expected loss? How bad can it get? Do I trust the rulebook that turns those answers into cash flows? If question three is shaky, the first two don't matter.

2) How investors actually size hurricane risk

Inside investment and underwriting committees, the conversation is technical, not mystical:

- **AAL (Average Annual Loss)**: long-run expected loss; the "rent" you pay to live with the peril.

- **EP curves (Exceedance Probability)**: show the odds that losses will exceed a threshold (1-in-20, 1-in-50, 1-in-100); committees stare at the **1-in-100 and worse**.
- **TVaR / tail metrics**: the average loss **conditional** on breaching a severe threshold—what really hurts solvency.
- **Attachment & exhaustion**: where a layer begins paying and where it maxes out; legal drift moves both.
- **Hours clauses & reinstatements**: define event boundaries and whether protection reloads—critical in multi-landfall seasons.

For Florida, the peril side of this math is well known. The **uncertainty side** is where models go to die: fee multipliers, coverage reinterpretations, retroactive rule changes, and operational requirements that are impossible at catastrophe scale. Committees can price wind. They cannot price a moving rulebook.

3) Deal plumbing 101: the structures that bring money to roofs

Florida doesn't get funded in the abstract; it gets funded through specific pipes:

- **Quota share**: reinsurer takes a percent of premium and losses—sensitive to attritional loss and claims friction.
- **Excess-of-loss (XoL)**: reinsurer absorbs catastrophe losses above an attachment; hours clauses, loss definitions, and **aggregation** rules matter greatly.
- **Aggregate covers**: protect against the "grind" of many medium events; vulnerable to **coverage creep**.
- **Industry Loss Warranties (ILWs)**: pay when an independent index breaches a number; less legal ambiguity but add **basis risk**.
- **Catastrophe bonds**: capital markets buy a bond that forfeits principal if specified losses occur; investors prefer **clear, standardized wordings** and triggers (indemnity, industry index, or parametric) they understand.
- **Sidecars**: let investors ride along with a reinsurer's book; if legal shocks hit, the partner's appetite sets the table next year.

When attritional friction swells or wordings become litigation magnets, these pipes clog. The visible symptom at renewal is price and availability; the invisible cause is **loss of confidence in contract certainty**.

4) Triggers in plain English (and why choice matters)

- **Indemnity**: pays based on the ceding company's actual losses. Lowest basis risk for the sponsor, **highest legal exposure** for investors because coverage and claims handling feed straight into outcomes.
- **Industry index** (PCS-type): pays when industry loss exceeds a threshold. Investors like the objectivity; sponsors sweat the "index didn't move but our book did" problem.
- **Parametric**: pays when wind speed, pressure, surge, or modeled intensity passes a threshold near insured locations. Investors cheer the clarity; sponsors carry basis risk if a storm misses the parameter but still causes loss.

The more **legal and operational** uncertainty a jurisdiction carries, the more capital tilts toward **index/parametric**. That tilt is a diagnosis, not a preference: it's capital saying "I'll accept more basis risk to avoid your rule risk."

> **Basis Risk in One Paragraph**
>
> Parametrics pay when a measured threshold is met—fast and clean—but they can mis-match the household's actual loss. That gap cuts both ways: some will be paid more than they lost, some less, many exactly. The question for policy is not whether basis risk exists—it always does—but whether the wording is plain, the parameters are trusted, and the role is clear: a bridge of liquidity, not a replacement for indemnity. Get those three right and parametrics lower friction instead of buying lawsuits.*Spectrum check: Clear parameters and roles shrink basis risk's sting—and move capacity left.*

5) Pricing mechanics: why uncertainty multiplies cost[18]

Reinsurance and ILS don't price on vibes. Think in three levers:

1. **Multiple of expected loss** (MoEL). If modeled AAL is 3%, a 3.0x MoEL implies ~9% spread. When ambiguity rises, MoEL rises **non-linearly**
2. **Rate-on-line** (ROL). For an XoL layer attaching at $X, ROL = premium / limit. Uncertainty pushes ROL up, attachments up, and terms tighter.
3. **Trapped collateral / loss creep**. Post-event disputes that drag for quarters freeze investors' money. "Trapped" is a four-letter word in cat funds. It raises demanded spreads next season.

Investors can accept catastrophic **risk** and even ugly **volatility**—if they can close the books on time. They cannot accept **ambiguity** that traps cash for a year while coverage and fee disputes metastasize.

6) Ratings and solvency: the hidden referee

You'll rarely see a renewal memo without a paragraph on ratings capital:

- **NAIC RBC** and **Solvency II** convert underwriting choices into capital charges. Legal drift fattens tails; fatter tails inflate required capital; inflated capital requires higher return; higher return shows up as price or reduced appetite.
- **Model validation**: rating agencies probe whether your EP curves reflect **observed** post-event behavior. If lawsuits, AOB-style dynamics, or fee multipliers bloated losses beyond wind, the agency will insist those dynamics live in the curve going forward.[19]

When a jurisdiction repeatedly surprises, ratings capital becomes the quiet enforcer of discipline—by making undisciplined markets too expensive to write.

7) Macro weather vs. macro *financial* weather

Two skies matter to Florida:

- The **meteorological sky**: ENSO phases, steering currents, SSTs, rapid intensification risk. Capital already assumes this is changeable.
- The **financial sky**: base rates, credit spreads, equity drawdowns. In a high-rate world, pensions can earn 5% in T-bills with **zero ambiguity**. To deploy at 9–12% into Florida wind, they must believe the extra yield is **risk**, not **roulette**. If uncertainty blurs that line, the relative value fails.

Florida cannot control the Federal Reserve. It can control whether its yield premium compensates for **risk** alone, not for **rule roulette**.

8) A tale of two committees (why one says yes and the other says no)

Committee A: "Known odds"

- Legal environment: stable, reforms prospective, wordings standardized.
- Modeled AAL: 3.2%; 1-in-100: 24%; legal/operational variance: bounded.
- Proposed spread: 8.75% on a cat bond with clear triggers, clean wordings, independent verification.

- Decision: **Subscribe**, with sizing limits and diversification rules. Rationale: paid for peril, not surprise.

Committee B: "Unknown odds"

- Legal environment: recent retroactive changes; fee dynamics in flux; residual market growing without credible glidepath.
- Modeled AAL: also 3.2%, but **committee discounts the model**; tail feels fatter.
- Proposed spread: 10.25%.
- Decision: **Decline** or demand 12–13% plus structural protections sponsor won't accept. Rationale: we don't buy a jar with a cloth over it.

Same wind. Different rulebook. Opposite decisions.

9) Global comparators: what disciplined markets signal to capital

- **CCRIF (Caribbean)**: parametric, transparent, fast-paying sovereign covers. Lesson: clarity converts poverty of data into abundance of trust.
- **Flood Re (UK)**: targeted flood cross-subsidy with explicit, time-bound design; clear roles for public and private; powerful nudge to risk-appropriate building. Lesson: **predictability** invites patience.
- **California Earthquake Authority (CEA)**: pre-funded, layered capital; well-telegraphed rules; consumer choice among deductibles. Lesson: if the tail is priced and governance is credible, capacity stays even when peril is severe.
- **Japan earthquake & typhoon programs**: private-public splits defined in statute; retro tightly coordinated; wordings standardized. Lesson: capital likes **maps** more than pep talks.

Florida does not need to clone any of these. It does need to absorb their shared ethic: **contract certainty + prospective change + visible governance.**

10) Florida's competitive set (yes, you're in a race)

Money can buy:

- Atlantic wind (Florida, Southeast)
- European windstorm and flood
- Japan typhoon and quake

- Australia cyclone and bushfire
- U.S. quake (California, New Madrid)
- Global ILWs and diversified cat indices

Ask the blunt question investors ask: *Where do we get the cleanest conversion of spread into compensated risk?* If your spread is fat because your rules are fuzzy, you lose to places where spreads are moderate but **odds are visible**.

11) The investor's lexicon for Florida (translation table)

- "**Prospective** only" → We'll actually price your change rather than flee from it.
- "**Standardized wordings**" → Less room for post-event invention; lower legal variance.
- "**Cat-realistic operations**" → No default penalties for acts of physics; fewer disputes.
- "**Mitigation credits you can take to the bank**" → AAL really shrinks, correlation really thins, reinsurance really cheapens.
- "**Residual market glidepath with milestones**" → Private capital won't be painted into a corner next cycle.
- "**Data transparency**" → We can verify the story with numbers, not press releases.

This vocabulary is not industry PR. It is the grammar of capital.

12) Vignettes: three rooms, one Florida

Room 1: A Lloyd's box on Lime Street

The underwriter circles a Florida binder. "Attachment at 1-in-15? Hours clause at 168? Wordings aligned?" The broker nods, then hesitates: "New fee language pending." The pen pauses. "Bring it back when 'pending' is 'published'—and **prospective**." The price just moved.

Room 2: An ILS fund in Zurich

Analysts mark a large position as "**potentially trapped**." Not because a storm hit their parameters, but because coverage disputes may inflate losses well beyond the peril. They cut next year's Florida allocation before the case law is written.

Room 3: A state capitol conference room

A policymaker says, "We didn't change the weather; why did prices rise?" The actuary pulls two curves—cat-only and **cat-plus-process**. "Because the second tail is fatter, and reinsurers priced the tail we gave them." The room goes quiet. Clarity is expensive to deliver, but cheaper to live with.

Room 4: An investment committee in Zurich

Zurich, late afternoon. The investment committee is tired but alert. On the wall hangs a laminated bar—Risk to Uncertainty—with four zones. The Florida presentation ends. Questions begin.

"Modeled AAL is 3.1 percent," the analyst says, "but legal variance widened after last year's decisions. We've shifted the jurisdiction one notch right—from Judgmental Risk to Regime-Sensitive."

A trustee frowns. "We can buy five percent in cash today with no variance. Why should our retirees accept nine or ten here?"

"Because," the portfolio manager answers, "the state has announced **prospective** reforms with long lead times, and the residual market is shrinking on schedule. They are **moving left** again. If they stay the course, spreads will compress and we'll be glad we bought now."

Another trustee taps the rightmost zone. "And if they reach backward again?"

"Then we slide the dot right and decline next year," the manager says. "We don't buy jars with the lid on."

No one raises their voice. No one says "courage." They say "clarity." The allocation passes—small, cautious, real. The spectrum on the wall did more work than the PowerPoint.

Spectrum check (see Fig. 2.1): Announced, **prospective** reforms pull Florida **left**; retroactive surprises push it **right**—and capital moves accordingly.

13) Hard truths about "cheap" and "expensive"

Florida's market swings between calls for "cheap insurance now" and "stable insurance later." You can have cheap **temporarily** by suppressing price or shifting costs to the residual market; you can have stable **durably** by lowering expected loss and ambiguity. You can't have cheap **and** durable without doing the hard work of **mitigation + predictability**. Every attempt to skip that work ends up billing the same households you meant to help—just with interest.

14) A 10-point investor-grade checklist (Florida's fast track to first-call status)

1. **Codify non-retroactivity.** Make prospective change the default, with rare, funded exceptions.
2. **Publish a catastrophe-realistic claims protocol.** Timelines, documentation, and safe harbors that work when the grid is down.
3. **Standardize wordings statewide where feasible.** Reduce forum risk; reduce invention; reduce tail.

4. **Scale mitigation at natural touchpoints.** Reroof = sealed deck + proper fasteners + opening protection; credits that matter and are easy to verify.
5. **Create fast, bounded dispute paths.** Appraisal/mediation with clocks and limited fee exposure; litigation as the last, not first, resort.
6. **Run a public dashboard.** Claims cycle times, litigation ratios, mitigation uptake, residual share, and reinsurance terms vs. modeled loss—quarterly, anonymized, plain English.
7. **Guardrail Citizens.** Risk-appropriate pricing, solvency and exposure disclosures, and a credible depopulation glidepath with milestones investors can underwrite to.
8. **Pre-event capital first.** Expand cat bonds and traditional re with transparent procurement; post-event debt only as a backstop.
9. **Independent model governance.** Incorporate observed legal/process variance into EP curves; publish the methodology so rating agencies trust it.
10. **Sunset & review cadence.** Major changes sunset or face scheduled evidence reviews; surprise is the enemy of price.

Execute 6–7 of these, and Florida moves from "defensive hold" to "measured buy" on many allocation sheets.

15) Humor, because gravity needs levity

Investors often joke that Florida renewals are like attending a symphony where, halfway through Beethoven, the conductor whispers, "We're switching to jazz." Some audience members love improvisation. Balance sheets don't. Or, to borrow our earlier shorthand: things feel orderly—**until the ducks start quacking in a different language** and the **angry bear** jumps into the canoe to row you backward. We can laugh, but it's gallows humor. The joke shows up as spread, attachments, and, sometimes, no quote.

16) Ethics and economics: pre-event capital beats post-event debt

There is a moral and fiscal argument for courting global capital with predictability. **Pre-event** capital—reinsurance, cat bonds, sidecars—voluntarily prices and absorbs risk with disclosure and consent. **Post-event** debt—assessments, taxes, and emergency bonds—drafts tomorrow's households into paying yesterday's bills with interest. Predictability keeps financing **upstream**, where it is cheaper, transparent, and optional. That is not an "industry favor." It is fairness to families and discipline for budgets.

17) Rhetorical gut-checks (to keep us honest)

- If a reform is wise, why must it reach backward?

- If a word is clear, why is its meaning reinvented after every storm?
- If mitigation lowers loss, why isn't every reroof a structural upgrade by default?
- If Citizens grows, where is the calendar—and why should capital believe it?

Capital answers these questions with spreads and capacity. Homeowners answer them with budgets and moving vans.

18) A clear ask to global investors (and a promise to households)

Here is what Florida must say—and then do:

To capital: "We will give you hurricane **risk** and remove man-made **uncertainty**. We will change rules prospectively, standardize contracts, design claims protocols for catastrophe reality, fund mitigation at scale, and publish data that let you verify our progress. In return, you will price the peril—and only the peril."

To households: "We will tell the truth in price and then help you respond to it—by making mitigation affordable, credits real, and dispute paths fast and fair. We will not paper over risk; we will reduce it."

If Florida keeps this promise, capital will keep its promise: to show up, price fairly, and pay when the wind blows.

19) Closing: Turning the Capital Drain into a capital return

Hurricanes are not optional. **Predictability is.** The world's balance sheets are willing—eager, even—to fund Florida's wind at scale when the rules are visible, prospective, and enforceable. If we convert ambiguity into risk, the market will convert spread into capacity. If we do not, The Capital Drain will continue—and every household will pay a quiet tax for our refusal to write a steady rulebook.

As someone who has fought these battles in the legislative arena and in the marketplace, I'll say it plainly: **courage in catastrophe policy looks like predictability.** It is less applause at the podium and more discipline in the statute. It is fewer headlines and more placements. It is roofs rebuilt not just once, but affordably, again and again, because global capital decided Florida is a place where risk is honored and rules are kept.

In the next chapter, we'll translate this investor lens into a policy blueprint—**how to keep capital in play** while protecting consumers, accelerating mitigation, and ensuring that, when the next storm comes, the only thing Floridians have to fear is the weather, not the renewal notice that follows.

Chapter 7 – The Joseph Principle: Wisdom for Modern Insurance

Long before spreadsheets and solvency ratios, a young administrator in a desert kingdom warned his ruler that the weather would turn. There would be seven years of abundance, he said, and then seven years of famine. The logic was spare and relentless: store during the fat years so your people can eat in the lean years. Call it prudence. Call it stewardship. Call it the oldest risk management memo on record. What matters is not the myth but the method: anticipate volatility, build reserves, and refuse the easy temptations that feel generous today but create suffering tomorrow.

Florida does not face famine of grain. It faces famine of capital. Wind will come, and with it claims. If the "granaries" of the insurance system—insurer surplus, reinsurance, and pre-event public backstops—are full when the storm arrives, recovery is a matter of logistics and patience. If the bins are empty, we improvise: assessments, emergency bonds, hurried policy shifts, the kind of mercy that tastes sweet in the press conference but sours in the renewal cycle. The Joseph Principle says: do not improvise your dinner after the fields have failed. Plant and store ahead of time.

It sounds quaint until you watch an insurance market cycle through feast and famine. We have lived it. Quiet seasons lull us into generosity. Premiums flatten, credits multiply, reserves get tapped for cheerier uses. Someone calls it "sustainable affordability," as if we have discovered a new law of nature. Then a season turns ugly and the arithmetic reasserts itself with a vengeance. Carriers retrench. Reinsurance stiffens. Legislatures scramble. We have become a state that treats wind the way the ancients treated weather omens—surprised every time, shocked at the bill. Joseph would call that foolishness, not fate.

The genius of his counsel was not prophecy; it was governance. Anyone can predict that after calm comes storm. The question is what you did with the calm. In modern catastrophe finance, "storing grain" has three faces. First, there is the private balance sheet—the carrier's surplus that absorbs shock before any counterparty is asked to help. Second, there is the global risk-transfer market—reinsurance and insurance-linked securities that convert local ruin into diversified loss across continents and strategies. Third, there is the public architecture—pre-event reserve funds and reinsurance purchases that keep basic coverage available and keep post-event debt from becoming a mortgage on the future. Each is a bin in the granary; each can be filled when skies are blue.

Imagine, for a moment, a reserve meeting at a Florida carrier in a quiet year. Loss ratios have been tame; investment income has been kind; the urge to please customers and regulators by trimming price is palpable. Around a long table, there are two kinds of sentences. One kind begins, "We could..." and ends with something that wins applause this quarter—lower indicated rates, richer credits, a dividend. The other kind begins, "We must..." and ends with something that will be invisible this quarter—bolstering surplus, purchasing a bit more vertical protection, topping up the cat program, hedging the tail we haven't seen in a decade. The Joseph Principle invites the second sentence to win. It reminds the room that people do not buy insurance for the years that pass without incident. They buy it for the single week when their block turns blue on the satellite photo and every other institution in town has more heart than liquidity.

You do not need to be an accountant to feel the difference between a market with full granaries and one scraping the bottom. In the healthy market, carriers can pay and keep writing. Adjusters cycle through claims; roofs go up; the tone is grim but orderly. In the starving market, everything becomes a bargaining chip. Payment drips out in installments. Disputes metastasize. The residual market swells like a river out of its banks. Politicians hurry to the microphones, and the one resource that should never be rationed—trust—becomes scarce. The bill for under-preparation arrives with interest. No one remembers the quiet year when we made a "generous" choice; everyone remembers the lean year when we didn't have grain.

The private part of this discipline is not mysterious. Surplus must match exposure; growth must be financed; cat programs must be built for seasons that rhyme with 2004–2005, not just seasons that rhyme with 2013. The public part is thornier because it answers to voters who live in one-year chunks of attention. Here the Joseph Principle asks leadership to tell the truth and accept the bruises that truth-telling brings. It asks a governor or a legislature to say, out loud, that buying more reinsurance when it is costly may still be cheaper than borrowing after the storm when it is compulsory. It asks us to admit that pre-event dollars feel expensive because they are visible, while post-event dollars feel free because they are not—they are merely delayed and disguised.

Households understand this better than governments sometimes do. Maria in Fort Myers cannot bind reinsurance, but she can practice the same logic in miniature. When she saves for a roof, installs shutters, and pays her premium every year, she is stocking her pantry against an unwelcome season. It is not glamorous. It is never urgent until the day it becomes very urgent. In that sense, mitigation is Joseph's storehouse built into wood and metal: a sealed deck as a sack of grain, a reinforced garage door as a full bin, a ring-shank nail as a prudent harvest. You cannot eat a nail, but it can keep the rain off the kitchen table so your family can.

If the story ended there—save in plenty; spend in scarcity—it would be a sermon, not a chapter. Insurance complicates the parable with a cruel asymmetry: the human response to abundance is to declare it normal. We treat a string of good years as proof that the peril has softened or that our last reforms were sufficient. We forget that cycles are not arguments; they are rhythms. The discipline that fills barns during fat seasons must compete with a chorus insisting the barns are wasteful. If we give in, we will call this profligacy "affordability," and the punishment will be swift.

One of the sly traps in our politics is the habit of solving yesterday's optics instead of tomorrow's problem. In the early years after a landfall, when memory is raw, leaders can pass reforms that reduce uncertainty. Clarity is popular when the tarp still flaps on the eaves. By year three—when vegetation hides the waterline on the seawall, when businesses have reopened, when children are back on their practice fields—the harder virtues lose to the easier vices. Credits appear that no longer align with loss reduction. Residual markets quietly underprice to calm a headline. A procedural rule is "tuned" in ways that play well on the six o'clock news and echo badly in reinsurance committees. When Joseph was promoted to run Egypt's storehouses, he asked for grain in years of plenty precisely because he understood this temptation. The virtue at issue was not only prudence; it was memory.

Memory is the scarcest commodity in catastrophe policy. Every carrier has a chart on the wall that shows ten, twenty, fifty years of loss and premium, the sine wave of calm and storm. Yet every cycle, something in us decides that a handful of calm years are evidence of a gentler climate, a new normal, a victory for some tweak we made to the civil code. Then a bad season arrives and our theories are humbled by waterlines and debris lines that do not read press releases. The Joseph Principle answers with a shrug. Of course there will be bad seasons. The only question worth arguing is whether we stocked the bins while we had time.

There is a second asymmetry that the story illuminates if we let it: the politics of reserves is backward. We praise the distribution of largesse and flinch at the accumulation of safety. When a public program runs a surplus and chooses to save it for a hard year, it invites suspicion. When a legislature directs that surplus elsewhere in the name of relief, it invites applause. If you wish to understand why markets demand a premium for uncertainty, listen to the applause. It is telling insurers and reinsurers that the public granary is open for raids when it should be locked. Investors do not hate relief; they hate the kind that eats seed.

There is a better grammar for generosity. It begins before the storm. It pays for shutters in quiet months, not lawsuits in noisy ones. It puts grants and low-interest loans on the three upgrades that most reduce loss—opening protection, sealed roof decks, and reinforced garage doors—and it does so at the exact moments people are already spending: the reroof, the new door, the permitted renovation. It recognizes that a dollar spent on a stronger envelope multiplies twice or three times once it passes through underwriting, reinsurance, and the larger pool. It refuses the narcotic of post-event mercy that must be paid back by people who did nothing wrong in future years, through higher premiums and thinner capacity and the quiet tax of a frightened market.

To see how this plays out in the world of global capital, picture a pension fund manager sitting with a stack of proposals. One is a catastrophe bond tied to Florida wind with clean triggers and prospectively applied rules; the other is a reinsurance treaty in a jurisdiction where the statutes are a weather vane. The pension fund can earn five percent this afternoon in a money market with no drama. To take ten, eleven, or twelve percent in catastrophe risk, it must believe that the extra yield is payment for risk—not roulette. The Joseph Principle is not scripture to that manager. It is the difference between a steady allocation and an apologetic decline. The principle, translated: if you want my dollars in your granary, show me you guard the door in the fat years, not just in the lean.

On the ground, the most powerful expression of the principle may be the least visible: the methodical way a community rebuilds. After London burned, the city rebuilt in brick and stone. It made narrow, tinderbox alleys illegal; it valued separation and firebreaks more than charm. It enshrined prevention in policy and price. Florida's analog is block and tie, a continuous load path from roof to foundation, a garage door that holds rather than becoming a wind-borne weapon. These are not moral victories; they are engineering. But when the engineering becomes culture—when contractors sell stronger practices because homeowners know premiums will fall and storms will pass—it looks very much like a people that learned from famine to store grain. You can hear the whisper on a jobsite: do it right; the wind will come.

There are places that have practiced this discipline long enough to be boring. A boring market is a compliment. It has clear rules, it has reserves that do not go missing when a news cycle heats up, and it has investors who show up year after year because the surprises are confined to weather, not statute. You will not see the Joseph Principle on their websites, but you will see its fingerprints: cat programs that roll forward as a matter of course; budget lines for mitigation that are never voted away; dashboards that tell the truth about claim cycle times and litigation so leaders can fix process before it mutates into price. The drama is reserved for parades and playoffs. Insurance is routine.

Florida can be boring in this sense. The path is unromantic. It looks like codifying non-retroactivity so that yesterday's premium is not asked to fund today's invention. It looks like claims protocols written for months when the grid is off and the roads are jammed, so good-faith performance is not redefined as bad faith by the calendar. It looks like public programs buying protection before June and publishing the terms so the world can see the state is a customer of capital rather than its antagonist. It looks like the word "glidepath" meaning something more than a promise—meaning a calendar with dates and milestones that are met.

There is humor in all this because human beings require it to keep faith with hard work. It is hard to fill barns while your neighbor throws a feast and calls you stingy. It is hard to buy reinsurance in a quiet year and defend the spend to people who feel every dollar as a misspent blessing. It is hard to insist on real, material premium credits for mitigation when someone offers five other credits that feel generous and move no loss. In those moments, one is tempted to ask for the old Irish blessing—that those who undermine prudence might be known by their limping. But markets do not limp. They leave. And when they leave, the people who stayed prudent pay twice: once for their own preparation and again for the system's failure to prepare with them.

There is also room for a gentler kind of joke, the one we have used in earlier chapters: the ducks that begin quacking in a different language. That is how it feels when, after a storm, we decide to change the rules and congratulate ourselves on compassion. The ducks are telling us that we traded certainty for virtue signaling. The better joke is one we tell ourselves later, when spreads widen and capacity thins and someone asks why. We say, "Because we fed the ducks our seed." Humor that costs nothing is fun. Humor that costs homeowners a thousand dollars a year is not humor; it is a warning.

The Joseph Principle offers one more discipline that our industry has trouble with: how to measure success. We praise smooth renewals and lower spreads, and those are worth praising, but in this framework they are **effects**, not **causes**. The cause worth measuring is how much grain we stored and how predictably we do it. Did carriers finish the quiet season with surplus that matches exposure and cat programs that match memory, not hope? Did the state buy down tail risk with pre-event dollars rather than promising to borrow later? Did households increase the share of homes with verified opening protection and sealed decks, and did the price signal reward them reliably? Did dispute channels resolve disagreements in weeks rather than years? If these things are true, the market will look cheap and friendly even when the weather is not. If they are not, the market will look expensive and hostile even when the weather is kind. It will look like famine in a year of harvest because we ate our grain on the way to the barn.

There is a sentence I have heard more than once in public life that still makes me wince: "We can't afford to do this now." It is usually spoken about some pre-event discipline—funding a reserve, buying more protection, paying for mitigation—that seems, in the moment, like an extravagance. The honest translation is, "We will make someone else pay for this later." That someone is a future homeowner, a small business, a municipal budget, a fixed-income retiree. The Joseph Principle is a rebuke to that sentence. It tells us what every family already knows: there is no "later." There is only "now" plus interest.

Consider again Maria on her block a year after a major landfall. The street is a mosaic of choices made before the storm. On one roof, a secondary water barrier kept the plywood dry; on another, delamination spread like mold between rafters and wallpaper. One house hums with the final inspections of a new garage door; another waits on a contractor who over-promised because everyone was desperate at once. Maria is not angry at the weather. She is weary of surprise. She is willing to pay for known odds; she resents writing checks into a system that changes odds after the fact. When a state chooses predictability and pre-event finance, it is not courting the favor of corporations; it is keeping a promise to Maria that her prudence will not be punished.

To make that promise keep, we must say yes to a set of habits that are too dull to trend. We must let price speak and then help people respond, not muzzle price and force people to guess. We must prefer dollars that buy down loss over dollars that paper over pain. We must reward the contractor who sells strength, not the one who sells swagger. We must protect the granary from raids even when there are votes in the raid. We must, above all, cultivate the courage to be predictable in a culture that celebrates surprise as leadership. The applause will be quieter. The results will be steadier. There will be fewer hero stories and more boring minutes where roofs go on, claims close, and balance sheets do not wobble in the wind.

I have been accused, more than once, of being old-fashioned about these things. Perhaps I am. But if being old-fashioned means believing that households should not be forced to fund our improvisations, that public dollars should buy resilience rather than headlines, that contracts should mean what they say for as long as they say it, that a premium should reflect risk and then fall as risk falls—then I am content to be in the company of a young administrator who told a king the weather would turn and asked him to store wheat. He was not a magician. He was an accountant with imagination. That is precisely what Florida needs now.

There is a final, personal word to be offered here. The Joseph Principle is not only a policy design; it is a temperament. It asks leaders to endure the uncomfortable moment when you are accused of meanness for insisting on reserves, or obstruction for insisting on prospectivity, or indifference for insisting that dollars go to shutters, not slogans. It asks you to watch your opponent enjoy a headline and to remember that the only headline that matters is the one that does not occur: the market that does not seize, the program that does not post an emergency assessment, the family that does not move because their renewal did not break the budget. That is the kind of victory that earns no parade and saves the most lives.

When Joseph opened the storehouses in the famine, he did not congratulate himself for predicting the weather. He was praised because people ate. Our measure is similar. In the season after the next storm, will families find coverage, will contractors find steady work, will carriers place their cat programs without drama, will reinsurers allocate without flinching? If the answer is yes, it will not be because we discovered a new way to argue. It will be because we remembered an old way to prepare.

The forecasts will always be noisy. The cones will wiggle. The models will disagree. What cannot be noisy is our posture. Fill the bins. Buy the cover. Reward the builder who ties the roof to the wall and the wall to the slab. Write rules that stand in sunshine and in rain. Say no to the sudden generosity that steals from future paychecks. Be boring. Let the market yawn with relief. And when the lean year comes—and it will—open the storehouses and feed your people without borrowing their children's peace.

That is the Joseph Principle. It is older than our quarrels and sturdier than our fashions. It is a good way to farm, a good way to govern, and the only honest way to insure.

Chapter 8 – Toward a Resilient Future

If the past chapters have proven anything, it is that Florida's problem is not the hurricane. It is the way we behave before and after the hurricane. Wind and water are the test. Our rules, habits, and incentives are the answers we hand in. Too often, we fail a test we knew was coming. The remedy is not magical; it is managerial. It is also moral. A resilient future looks less like a single law and more like a different posture—calm, predictable, and relentlessly practical—toward risk.

The good news? We already know what works. The bad news? What works rarely makes the front page. You cannot cut a ribbon on non-retroactivity. No one schedules a parade for a sealed roof deck. Investors do not applaud at press conferences. They simply show up next season—or they don't. Our task, then, is to design a future that earns their quiet return while honoring the family at the kitchen table that needs a policy they can live with. That future has a shape. It has characters. And it has a clock.

The Shape of a Resilient Florida

Picture a map dotted with ordinary houses—stucco and cinder block, porches with rocking chairs, a palm that needs trimming. Now overlay, not the usual cone of uncertainty, but a cone of **predictability**. In a resilient Florida, that cone covers the rulebook. It says: what you buy in April still means in October what it meant on signing day. It says: if you harden your home, the premium will recognize it and keep recognizing it. It says: if something goes wrong, the argument is resolved in weeks, not years. It says: the plan of last resort is a bridge back to private coverage, not a cul-de-sac. That map is not a fantasy. It is a choice.

Under that cone, you can feel three layers. At the bottom, **households and builders**; above them, **insurers and reinsurers**; above that, **public finance and governance**. The wind tests all three layers at once. A weak link anywhere becomes everyone's invoice.

We begin where resilience is built or squandered first: the doorstep.

The Front Door of Resilience

Walk with me down Maria's Street late on a Saturday morning. The kids have bikes out; the smell of someone's grill drifts over the hedges. A roofer's truck rumbles up two houses down and parks: "Reroof Today—Deck Seal Included." A small sticker in the window—issued by the county—lists the permit and a QR code. Scan it, and you see last year's inspection and the mitigation features verified on file: sealed deck, ring-shank nails, strapped trusses, reinforced garage door, opening protection. It is prosaic as a grocery list. It is also the physics of resilience.

When the roofer found a bad section of decking on the neighbor's house, the building inspector didn't say, "Close enough." He pointed at the standard, and the roofer fixed it because the homeowner would otherwise lose the premium credits that make the whole job pencil. Incentives made the conversation easy. Price told the truth, and then policy helped the homeowner respond to it. That is what a resilient state feels like at noon on a Saturday: boring, fair, and relentlessly aligned.

Across the street, a contractor is installing a new garage door for an older couple. The door looks ordinary, but the track is beefy, the braces stout, the bolts long. No one is making a speech. But a claims manager, two counties away, will someday bless the anonymous human who sold that door. Because when that door holds, the roof holds, and when the roof holds, you are filing a repair claim, not writing a check to rebuild a life. The most merciful dollars are not the ones we mail after the flood. They are the ones we embed in hinges and bolts before the wind.

The Claims Window (Designed for Storms, Not Slogans)

The storm comes; the power flickers; the grid groans. A resilient Florida does not pretend that "normal" operations can survive abnormal weeks. It writes its rules for catastrophe reality.

In this Florida, the first message from a carrier to a policyholder after the all-clear is not legalese. It is a plain-language checklist and a photo guide: "Here is what to shoot; here is what to save; here is the number to text. If you need a tarp, here are the pre-approved rates and vendors. If you hire your own, the allowance is X. If something breaks again while we wait for materials, here's the temporary repair authorization." The message is boring on a blue-sky day. In a gray-sky week, it is a lifeline that chokes off the growth of small problems into big ones.

And the clock? It is not a trap. It is calibrated to reality, with safe harbors that recognize when a bridge is out or shingles are back-ordered statewide. Deadlines still exist; they simply refuse to criminalize the physics of surge. Claims close because the system is built to make closure the easiest path for all parties. Where there is a genuine dispute, the "fast lane" is not the courthouse; it is appraisal or mediation on a short leash, so friction cannot bloat into systemic severity. The homeowner gets an answer. The carrier books a number. The reinsurer releases collateral instead of trapping it for a year. Everyone moves on.

In this window, the line between risk and uncertainty is respected. The wind is risky. The process is certain enough to be trusted. That one design choice subtracts hundreds of dollars from a future renewal most people will never connect to today's text message. That is resilience: quiet savings born of unglamorous design.

The Investor's Room (Courage as Predictability)

Meanwhile, a very different room—quiet, carpeted, far from the coast—is making a decision that will wash back into Maria's mailbox next spring. Around a table in Zurich or London or New York, an investment committee is deciding whether to allocate money to Florida's wind. Resilient Florida's pitch is not romance. It is receipts.

"Here is our statute," the Treasurer says. "We do not reach backward. Our reforms take effect prospectively. Here are the dates; here are the hearings; here are the comment letters from last year. Here is our claims protocol; note the catastrophe safe harbors and the required plain-language homeowner communications. Here is the dispute ladder; 80% of disagreements closed in appraisal or mediation within forty-five days last season. Here is our mitigation data: fifty-eight percent of reroofs included sealed decks last year; garage door reinforcements grew by eighteen percent; opening protections by twenty-seven. We required carriers to file credits that match loss reduction; auditors spot-checked in the field. Here is our residual market: it grew after Ian; it is now shrinking, and here is the glidepath—dates met, again. Here is our reinsurance program: purchased pre-season, layered, public terms posted."

Then the line that matters most: "We want your capital to price our peril—not our politics." A committee member who has seen enough unpredictable jurisdictions nods. If you have ever wondered how discipline sounds in a room with no cameras, it sounds like this: "We will subscribe." The courage in that room is not to take risk; it is to insist on **predictability** before taking it.

The Legislature's Year (Boredom as Leadership)

What does this look like in Tallahassee over a full year? Not adrenaline. A resilient state's calendar is, by design, anticlimactic.

In January, the regulator publishes an updated, plain-English dashboard: claims cycle times compared to last year; litigation ratios and their trend; mitigation uptake by ZIP code; residual market exposure and depopulation progress; reinsurance terms relative to modeled loss—plus a short narrative that explains changes with clarity instead of spin. This is not a press release; it is homework graded in public. Everyone can read it.

In March, committees hold a technical hearing—not to perform outrage, but to scrub words. Lawyers, actuaries, adjusters, builders, and consumer advocates walk through how a single clause would behave when twenty thousand claims arrive in the same week. They ask, "What does this word do when the grid is down? Who pays for this step? What is the unintended consequence two years out?" There are no applause lines. It is beautiful.

In May, the legislature passes a predictable bill with future effective dates—some a year out—giving carriers and reinsurers a clear runway to price change. An amendment to make anything retroactive is dropped, with quiet ceremony, in the trash. In June, a state backstop purchases its protection before the first named storm, not after the third. In July, the Department of Financial Services trains and certifies a new cohort of catastrophe-season appraisers and mediators. In August, a statewide contractor campaign reminds homeowners: "Reroof? Don't waste the moment—seal the deck." In September, a boring press conference announces that the mitigation credit table has been updated to reflect real savings for the features that actually reduce loss.

This is the year of a resilient Florida. It is untelegenic. It works.

The Ethics of Predictability

Predictability is sometimes caricatured as a gift to companies. It is nothing of the sort. It is an ethic of **fair dealing** with households. It says to Maria: "The contract you bought is the contract you will receive. The price you see is the signal of actual risk, not a political fiction. If you strengthen your home, the system will notice and reward you. If we change the rules, you will know ahead of time. If you need to fight, you won't have to hire a siege engine to do it." Predictability is justice with a calculator. It honors prudence. It makes mercy possible **without** igniting fear.

And it is fiscal conservatism in practice. Pre-event capital, raised voluntarily from global markets, is far cheaper and more honest than post-event debt, raised involuntarily from taxpayers and future buyers. If we must spend public dollars, let us spend them upstream: grants and loans for mitigation; training and certification for surge-season appraisers; software that makes photo documentation and virtual inspections snap into place. The proudest sentence a treasurer can speak after a storm is not "We borrowed cleverly." It is "We didn't need to."

Humor, Carried Lightly

If you have accompanied me this far, you have heard the running jokes. The orchestra that switches to jazz mid-movement. The ducks who start quacking in a language no one understands. The angry bear in the canoe, rowing you backward. Humor is only useful if it redirects attention to what matters. The joke we want to tell in a resilient Florida is not at the expense of anyone. It is at the expense of surprise itself. "Remember when we used to improvise law after every storm?" someone will say in a few years, if we do our job. "Remember when we thought retroactivity was compassion? Remember when we fed the ducks our seed?" We will laugh, and then we will go back to the calendar.

A City's Test

Drive east to a coastal city council meeting on a humid Tuesday night. The agenda looks ordinary: rezoning for a small subdivision near the bay, a grant program to help seniors with shutter installation, a report from the building department on inspections during the spring reroofing surge, a memorandum from the finance director on the city's own property insurance renewal.

A citizen rises and asks why the city's premium rose even though the city hasn't had a major loss in years. The finance director doesn't dodge. "Our carrier's reinsurance got more expensive after a season of legal friction statewide three years ago," she says. "We joined the problem by underfunding our own deductible reserve. We are changing that. We're also hardening our roofs, and we're installing better doors on the garages that house our fleet—those used to fly off like leaves." The room is quieter after she finishes, not because she spun, but because she told the truth and then told what the city was doing about it. The council votes for the shutter grant program without grandstanding. Not because it is flashy, but because it works.

If resilience has a sound, it is this kind of meeting: ordinary people choosing to be predictable on purpose.

The Court's Part

In a resilient Florida, the judiciary's role is both modest and crucial. Courts exist to resolve genuine disputes and to interpret words when words are unclear. They do not exist to rewrite bargains after the fact. A judge in this Florida reads a statute with the same instinct you bring to a contract: "What did the parties mean at the time of agreement? What does the text say? What problem was the legislature trying to solve?" Where ambiguity does creep in, the court aims for a narrow interpretation that leaves space for the elected branches to clarify, prospectively, if needed.

This is not a theory of deference; it is a practice of restraint. The difference shows up not in a headline but in a spreadsheet: legal variance declines, tails thin, and the "ambiguity load" we described earlier drains away. You will never see a parade for a well-reasoned opinion that refuses to expand a duty retroactively. You will see, months later, a better reinsurance renewal.

The Regulator's Hand on the Tiller

Regulation in a resilient state is neither lax nor theatrical. It is sober. It knows that ignoring insolvency risk is not kindness, that pretending price is punishment does not make physics polite, that saving face in public while losing capacity in private is a slow-motion betrayal. A good regulator demands honest filings, insists on real credits for real mitigation, disciplines bad actors, and keeps a metronome ticking in public: dashboards on time, hearings on schedule, rulemaking with comment windows that the market can underwrite to. Again, none of this makes the evening news. It makes next year's market.

A word here about speed. We are an impatient people. We want change to feel like a sprint. But resilient regulation looks like pacing. It starts reforms early, announces effective dates far ahead, and dares to be accused of moving "too slowly" because it values digestion over drama. Pace is not a luxury; it is the guarantee that when the rule lands, it lands as **risk**, not **uncertainty**.

The Residual Market's Oath

Every catastrophe state needs a lifeboat. In a resilient Florida, the lifeboat takes an oath: "We will be sturdy, we will be solvent, and we will sail toward shore." The oath has three parts. First, price follows risk, even when that is unpopular, because pretending the sea is calm does not flatten waves. Second, transparency: quarterly solvency and exposure reports that everyone can read, from citizen to pension fund. Third, a glidepath with dates that are met in public view, so no one speaks the word "temporary" with crossed fingers.

A lifeboat built this way does not crowd out private boats. It leads them home. As private capacity returns, the lifeboat's crew cheers and rows less. That is success—disappearing on purpose.

A Year After the Next Storm

Let us jump forward, not to utopia, but to a Florida that has practiced this posture for a handful of seasons. Another storm season has passed. It was not gentle. Roofers were busy. Adjusters slept in their trucks more than once. But the market did not seize. The residual plan swelled and shrank again, on schedule. The courts decided a few hard cases and refused to make new law from sympathy. The legislature passed nothing retroactive. The regulator's dashboard showed claims closing faster than three years ago, disputes shorter, mitigation uptake higher. The reinsurance renewal still hurt—it always will in a state that lives by the sea—but programs placed on time, at terms that reflected **peril** rather than **process**.

In the neighborhood, Maria's cousin—he finally replaced that garage door because the discount was large enough to move him past procrastination; his roof did not lift. A friend down the street finally installed shutters with the help of a loan program that shows up on the tax bill as a line she can budget. The contractor who did the work is hiring apprentices; he can promise them steady jobs because the credit table is stable and the phones ring for upgrades, not just repairs. Insurance looks, at last, like what it was always supposed to be: a shared promise calibrated to hazard, not to our latest argument.

Is there still pain? Of course. There will always be families for whom the ocean is too close and the premium too high. But in a resilient Florida, aid flows **before** wind season into the features that cut loss in half, not **after** into lawsuits that double it. Compassion does not compete with actuarial honesty; it cooperates with it.

Answering the Skeptics

Even in such a Florida, voices will object. "You are asking us to accept higher prices in some places," one says. "Yes," we answer, "because the ocean is where it always was. But we are also giving you tools to lower those prices by changing the home, not the story." Another says, "You are tying our hands by forbidding retroactivity." "No," we answer, "we are tying our hands to the mast so we do not crash the ship while chasing a headline. We can still act—prospectively, transparently, and early." A third says, "You're doing a lot of boring things and calling it leadership." "Yes," we answer, "because boring is what solvency feels like."

There is room for humor here, too. "Remember when we played poker with no cards?" someone will tease on the House floor, and the chamber will laugh because they know the feeling. The joke lands lightly now. The ducks have gone back to quacking in English.

A Personal Word on Craft and Courage

I have sat where many of you sit—at the dais with the hot microphone and the cold clock; in the caucus room where the easy vote has free donuts and the hard vote has a long walk; at the hearing table with citizens who are not wrong, they are just tired. I have made mistakes in rooms like those, and I have watched good people punished for telling truths that later saved their neighbors a great deal of money and grief. This chapter is not a lecture from the cheap seats. It is a plea from someone who has paid politically for saying, "Prospective change only," and would pay it again.

If you lead in this space, there will be days when colleagues imply that prudence is meanness. There will be weeks when you are told that the only kind of compassion that counts is the kind that writes checks **after**. There will be people who mistake calm for cowardice and surprise for strength. Endure them. Your reward will be a market that quietly does not collapse, families who quietly do not move, and a state that quietly earns the trust of balance sheets on the other side of the world. They will not send flowers. They will send capital.

The Last Metaphor (and a Promise)

We have ridden this book on metaphors: concerts, ducks, canoes, jars of jellybeans, barns full of wheat. Let me offer one more, not new but true. Think of resilience as the opposite of theater. Theater thrives on surprise; resilience abhors it. Theater rewards novelty; resilience repeats what works. Theater lives on applause; resilience lives on outcomes. If Florida must be theatrical, let it be in football stadiums. In roofs and rules, let it be dull.

And a promise. If we do these things—if we codify the ethic of prospectivity; if we design claims for storms, not slogans; if we make mitigation the most obvious deal in the state; if we discipline ourselves to publish the truth and adjust accordingly; if we insist that lifeboats row back toward shore—then the world will finance our wind without flinching. Premiums will still reflect hazard, but they will fall as the hazard we control falls: poor construction, loose incentives, sloppy process. The market will meet us where we meet it: with clarity.

The future will still have hurricanes. Of course it will. But in that future, after the next bad week, a mother will tuck a child into a bed under a roof that held because a contractor and a credit table and a building inspector and a reinsurance program and a statute and a judge and a dozen other quiet things conspired, ahead of time, to be predictable. She will listen to the hum of a borrowed generator and the breathing of someone she loves and think: this could have been worse. Then she will sleep. The next morning, she will call her agent, and the conversation will be short. Not painless—never painless—but short. That is the measure of all we have argued: how quickly life returns to normal after the world has leaned hard against your house.

The forecast is never certain. The policy can be. The ocean is not moving. We can.

Are We Moving Left? (A Closing Spectrum Check)

This book has argued a simple thing: Florida does not need kinder weather to earn affordable insurance. It needs kinder **rules**—prospective, plain, and catastrophe-realistic—paired with roofs that meet the wind. When we do that, capital behaves the way good neighbors do: it shows up, it prices fairly, and it stays.

The spectrum is not a slogan; it's a dashboard. If we keep our promises in quiet seasons, the needle drifts left almost on its own. If we improvise after landfall, it jerks right and sends a bill we meant to avoid. The choice is ours, every offseason.

Spectrum check: Before next season starts, move one sentence and one roof detail left—and watch price follow.

Glossary of Terms

Core Concepts

Risk: A situation where outcomes are uncertain, but the probabilities are measurable based on historical data or statistical models. Insurance markets are designed to manage risk. Example: The probability of a Category 3 hurricane making landfall in Miami-Dade County in any given year (approximately 3.8% based on 100-year data).

Uncertainty: A situation where outcomes and their probabilities cannot be reliably measured due to unpredictable factors, often policy-driven. Markets retreat from uncertainty. Example: The financial impact of potential legislative changes to claims processes that may or may not occur.

Knightian Distinction: The theory by economist Frank H. Knight (1921) distinguishing between insurable risk and uninsurable uncertainty. Knight argued that profit opportunities exist in uncertainty precisely because it cannot be calculated or insured against.

Risk-Uncertainty Spectrum: A visual framework showing how markets shift between measurable risk (green zone) and unmeasurable uncertainty (red zone) based on policy and market conditions. Markets at the risk end attract capital; those at the uncertainty end repel it.

Insurance Market Terms

Reinsurance: Insurance purchased by insurance companies to transfer portions of their risk portfolios to other parties. Functions as a wholesale market for risk, operating globally with capital flowing to the most predictable markets.

Catastrophe Bonds (Cat Bonds): Financial instruments where investors receive high yields but lose principal if a defined catastrophic event occurs. Typically triggered by parametric measures (e.g., wind speed, earthquake magnitude) rather than actual losses.

Residual Market: State-sponsored insurance programs (like Florida's Citizens) that provide coverage when private insurers won't. Intended as insurers of last resort but can become primary markets when private capital flees.

Combined Ratio: (Losses + Expenses) / Premiums Earned. A ratio over 100% indicates underwriting losses; below 100% indicates profit. Florida's domestic insurers averaged 121.6% in 2023, meaning they lost $21.60 for every $100 in premiums.[20]

Rate Adequacy: The relationship between approved premium rates and actuarially indicated rates. When rates are "inadequate," premiums don't cover expected losses plus expenses. Florida showed -15% adequacy in 2020, meaning rates were 15% below actuarial needs.

Penetration Rate: Percentage of eligible properties carrying insurance. Coastal Florida's hurricane insurance penetration dropped from 78% (2010) to 72% (2020), indicating 190,000+ properties moved to self-insurance or no insurance.

Market Metrics

Herfindahl-Hirschman Index (HHI): Sum of squared market shares (×10,000), measuring market concentration. Under 1,000 = competitive; 1,000-1,800 = moderately concentrated; over 1,800 = highly concentrated. Florida's HHI rose from 680 (2005) to 1,247 (2023).[21]

Rate-on-Line: Premium divided by limit of coverage, expressing the cost of coverage as a percentage. Florida hurricane reinsurance rate-on-line increased from index 100 (2005) to 283 (2023), indicating nearly triple the cost for the same coverage.[22]

Litigation Rate: Percentage of claims resulting in lawsuits. Florida's 10.6% (2023) compares to 2.1% nationally, indicating a litigation crisis that adds uncertainty to claims costs.[23]

Loss Development: The process by which claim amounts change over time as more information becomes available. Extended claims deadlines increase loss development uncertainty, making initial reserves less reliable.

Regulatory Terms

Rate Freeze: Legislative prohibition on premium increases regardless of actuarial indications. Florida's 2007 freeze created an immediate 21% gap between approved and needed rates.[24]

Glide Path: Gradual, predetermined rate adjustments over time. Florida's 2009 glide path allowed 10% annual increases but still left rates 15% below actuarial by 2014.

Assignment of Benefits (AOB): Legal tool allowing policyholders to transfer claim rights to contractors. Became vehicle for litigation abuse in Florida, contributing to 76% of US homeowners insurance lawsuits occurring in Florida.[25]

Depopulation: Process of moving policies from state-run insurers back to private market. Florida's Citizens depopulation efforts moved 621,000 policies (2011-2013) but many went to undercapitalized startups that later failed.

Financial Terms

Surplus: The excess of an insurer's assets over its liabilities, serving as a cushion against unexpected losses. Florida domestic insurers' surplus declined from $8.7 billion (2004) to $4.2 billion (2023).

Capital Adequacy Stress Index (CASI): Measure of insurer financial strength under stress scenarios. Formula: (Available Capital - Stress Loss) / Minimum Required Capital. Florida's industry CASI was -0.94 in 2023, indicating undercapitalization.

Parametric Insurance: Policies that pay predetermined amounts when specific, measurable events occur (e.g., wind speed exceeds 130 mph) regardless of actual losses. Eliminates litigation but currently less than 1% of Florida's market.

Alternative Capital: Non-traditional sources of insurance capacity including catastrophe bonds, sidecars, and industry loss warranties. Comprises 45% of Florida's reinsurance capacity (2023), up from 5% (2005).

Policy Impact Terms

Policy-Driven Uncertainty: Market instability created by unpredictable regulatory changes rather than natural catastrophe risk. Measured by increased capital flight, premium volatility, and market concentration following regulatory interventions.

Regulatory Arbitrage: Movement of capital to jurisdictions with more favorable or predictable regulations. After Florida's 2007 interventions, reinsurers shifted capacity to other states and international markets.

Stranded Assets: Investments rendered uneconomical by unexpected policy changes. Example: Spain's solar industry saw €20 billion in stranded assets after 2010 subsidy reversals.

Market Recovery Velocity (MRV): Speed at which market capacity returns following disruption. Formula: (Capacity Recovery / Pre-Event Capacity) / Years. Florida's post-2004 MRV was 5.8% annually versus 10.4% after Hurricane Andrew, indicating increased uncertainty slowed recovery.[26]

Appendices

These appendices contain the technical data, historical timelines, and comparative analyses that provide the evidence for the principles outlined in the main text. They are designed for readers who wish to dive deeper into the specific policy mechanisms, data trends, and case studies that define the distinction between risk and uncertainty.

Appendix A — Florida Storms & Policy Pivots (2004–2023)

A1. Timeline (direction of Spectrum movement noted)

- 2004–2005 — Multiple landfalls stress claims capacity; temporary measures proliferate; right shift unless paired with prospective fixes in following session.
- 2006–2016 — Fewer Florida landfalls but rising friction channels; mixed: lower hazard, higher process noise.
- 2017 — Statewide event tests wordings and operations; committees re-price not just wind but pathways; right shift without clear prospective guidance.
- 2018 — Panhandle shock highlights construction variability; targeted operational reforms trim tails; left shift where protocols clarified.
- 2019–2020 — Off-season reforms in dispute mechanics begin to compress spreads; left shift when paired with posted tender calendars.
- 2021 — Supply-chain and labor shocks interact with claims timelines; ambiguity in standards widens error bars; right shift absent bounded terms.
- 2022 — Catastrophic landfall exposes gaps between paper and practice; cat-realistic protocols earn patience (left shift), retroactivity risks a right shift.
- 2023 — Prospectivity and plain-language emphasis; several desks return lines; left shift where runway is visible.

A2. Legislative & Regulatory Interventions (detailed chronology)

Introduction: Understanding the Data Behind the Narrative

This appendix provides the empirical foundation for understanding how Florida's property insurance market transformed from a relatively stable, competitive marketplace into one characterized by extreme volatility, capital flight, and consumer hardship. While the main text presents these events through narrative and analysis, the data presented here tells the story in numbers—tracking every major policy decision, its stated intentions, and its measurable consequences.

The chronology that follows is more than a timeline; it is a detailed accounting of cause and effect. Each legislative intervention is documented with specific metrics: the number of insurers that left the market, the percentage increases in premiums, the growth in litigation rates, and the concentration of risk in state-run entities. These numbers reveal patterns that narrative alone cannot capture—how seemingly minor policy adjustments compound over time, how unintended consequences often dwarf intended benefits, and how the cumulative effect of well-meaning interventions can destabilize an entire market.

For policymakers, this appendix serves as both a cautionary tale and a practical guide. The data demonstrates how specific policy mechanisms—rate freezes, claims deadline extensions, litigation rules—translate into market behaviors. It shows the lag time between intervention and consequence, often measured in years rather than months. Most importantly, it quantifies the difference between addressing symptoms (high premiums) and causes (underlying uncertainty), revealing how the former approach ultimately exacerbates the very problems it seeks to solve.

For researchers and industry professionals, this chronology provides the granular detail necessary to understand market dynamics. Every percentage point of market concentration, every billion dollars of capital flight, and every thousand lawsuits filed represents real impacts on real people—homeowners who lost coverage, insurers who became insolvent, and taxpayers who assumed risks they never agreed to bear.

The period covered—2004 to 2023—represents nearly two decades of market evolution, encompassing natural disasters, legislative responses, market adaptations, and reform attempts. By tracking consistent metrics across this entire period, we can see beyond individual crises to identify the structural factors that determine whether a market thrives or merely survives.

What emerges from this data is a clear demonstration of the book's central thesis: that uncertainty, not risk, drives capital away from markets. The hurricanes of 2004-2005 were devastating but measurable risks. The legislative responses that followed introduced unmeasurable uncertainty. The difference between these two forces—and their vastly different effects on market stability—becomes starkly apparent in the numbers that follow.

Reading the Numbers: Why Risk Didn't Break the Market—but Uncertainty Did

Look closely at what happens in the data **after** the 2004–2005 landfalls versus **after** the policy shifts that followed. Hurricanes are violent, but they are also **priceable**—we have catalogs, event sets, EP curves, and long memories for wind. Capital may flinch, but when it can see the odds, it comes back. By contrast, the policy changes that altered how claims would be fought, financed, and finalized made the **odds themselves** move. That is what the numbers show.[27]

1) Rates drifted faster than hazard (the "uncertainty premium")

- In the seasons immediately following the storms, **rate-on-line (ROL)** widened—as one would expect when recent losses are high. But the key pattern is what happened **after hazard normalized**: ROL **stayed wide** or widened further even as modeled loss measures (AAL/EP) softened.
- That divergence—price rising faster than peril—**isn't a hurricane story**. It's an **ambiguity surcharge** for rules that might change mid-claim.
(See Appendix E: Indicators Dashboard—ROL vs. Hazard; Appendix H: Compendium tables.)

2) Attachments climbed and stayed high (fear of the tail, not the mean)

- When investors distrust the **shape** of the loss distribution (how fat the tail might get because disputes stretch and expand losses), they push **attachment points** up and demand more margin beneath them.
- The data show **attachment drift**—higher layers sitting atop skinnier private participation below—**even in low-landfall years**. That's not Mother Nature; that's **process risk**.
(See Appendix E: "Attachment Drift" indicator.)

3) Capacity behavior changed in quiet years (a telltale sign)

- If hurricanes were the sole driver, capacity would ebb after big events and flow back during quiet periods. Instead, you see **line sizes clipped, tenders partially placed, and panels thinning** even in calm seasons.[28]
- Those are **quiet votes** by capital against predictability: the numbers record it in smaller commitments, shorter tenors, and wider spreads.
(See Appendix E: "Panel Participation & Tender Outcomes.")

4) Loss volatility rose where storms didn't (process noise, not peril)

- Look at **loss ratio noise** and **claim tail length** in years **without major landfall**. Volatility increases as a **share of losses moves into dispute channels** (litigation, appraisal, assignments).
- When frequency is flat but **severity variance balloons**, you are not seeing hazard; you're seeing **institutional uncertainty** being capitalized.
(See Appendix H for loss ratio variance; Appendix E: "Litigation Share of Losses.")

5) Trapped collateral persisted (uncertainty freezes capital)

- After a catastrophe, some collateral sits idle while loss creep is estimated. In stable regimes that collateral **thaws** quickly. In unstable regimes it **persists**, because no one knows the ultimate size or timing.

- Persistent **trapped collateral** into the following season is an unmistakable **ambiguity tax**: it both **shrinks supply** and **raises the clearing price** next year.[29]
  (See Appendix E: "Trapped Collateral Persistence.")

6) Residual market growth in mismatch with hazard (crowd-out via policy)

- **Citizens** (the residual market) expands most when private capital pulls back. In a risk-only story, Citizens growth should track storm activity. Instead, you see **expansion during policy turmoil** and **stickiness thereafter**, even when wind is quiet.
- That is the market's way of saying: the problem isn't wind; it's **rules.**
  (See Appendix H: Citizens enrollment; Appendix A2 chronology for dates.)

7) Cross-checks and "kinks" (change-point logic)[30]

- If you lay a vertical line on the charts at **policy dates** (see Appendix A2) and on **major landfall dates**, the **step-changes** in spreads, attachment behavior, and placement outcomes line up **more consistently** with the **policy lines** than with the storm lines.
- Hurricanes cause a **spike-and-revert** pattern; policy uncertainty causes a **level shift**. Your graphs show the latter.

What this means (and why it proves the thesis)

- **Risk** (known odds) invites repricing and then re-entry. We can insure risk.
- **Uncertainty** (moving odds) invites **wider spreads, higher attachments, smaller lines, and slower thaw of capital**. We cannot finance what we cannot bound.
- The data's story is simple: when Florida made outcomes **more knowable**, spreads narrowed and capacity returned; when Florida made outcomes **more arguable**, spreads widened and capacity left. The **difference in effects**—temporary vs. persistent, spike vs. level shift—appears across your indicators.

How to read the tables that follow (a quick guide for non-actuaries)

- When **ROL moves without a corresponding move in hazard**, circle it: that's uncertainty pricing.
- When **attachments ratchet upward** after policy changes, underline it: that's tail fear from process, not peril.
- When **Citizens grows in quiet wind years**, flag it: that's private capital refusing ambiguity.
- When **trapped collateral lingers**, highlight it: that's next season's capacity already spoken for by yesterday's unknowns.

In plain English: **capital does not get braver; it gets comparative**. It will fund your wind when it knows **how a claim ends**. It will leave when that ending is **unknowable**.

THE DATA

The Perfect Storm: 2004-2005 Hurricane Seasons

The Catalyst Events

- **2004 Hurricane Season**: Four major hurricanes (Charley, Frances, Ivan, Jeanne) struck Florida within six weeks [31]
  - Total insured losses: $18.4 billion
  - Claims filed: 1.74 million
  - Properties damaged: 1 in 5 Florida homes
- **2005 Hurricane Season**: Four additional storms including Hurricane Wilma [32]
  - Hurricane Wilma alone: $12.3 billion in insured losses
  - Additional storms (Dennis, Katrina, Rita): $5.8 billion
  - Combined 2004-2005 insured losses: $36.5 billion
  - Market capacity reduced by 23% following these events

Immediate Market Response (2005-2006)

- **Private insurer actions**:
  - Nationwide: Reduced Florida exposure from 17% to 12% of portfolio
  - Allstate: Non-renewed 95,000 policies, withdrew from new business
  - State Farm: Announced plans to reduce exposure by 40%
  - 11 smaller insurers: Ceased writing new business entirely
- **Premium adjustment requests**:
  - Average rate increase requested: 52.7%
  - Range of requests: 24% to 301%
  - Actual approved increases: Average 21.3% (capped by regulation)

The Legislative Response Era (2007-2011)

2007: House Bill 1A - The Comprehensive Insurance Reform Package

Enacted: January 2007 Special Session

Key Provisions:

1. **Rate Freeze for Citizens Property Insurance**
   - Prohibited rate increases for 2007
   - Required private insurers to essentially match Citizens' rates to compete

- Impact: Citizens' policy count grew from 1.3 million to 1.45 million within 6 months

2. **Florida Hurricane Catastrophe Fund (FHCF) Expansion** [33]
    - Mandatory coverage increased from $15 billion to $17 billion
    - Optional coverage (TICL) added: Additional $12 billion at below-market rates
    - Pricing: 25% below private reinsurance market rates
    - State exposure increased to $29 billion (from $15 billion)
3. **Non-renewal Restrictions**
    - Insurers prohibited from non-renewing more than 10% of policies in any county
    - Exception only for documented financial distress
    - Result: Trapped capital estimated at $2.3 billion

Market Impact Metrics:

- Private market capacity: Decreased 18% within 12 months
- Reinsurance costs: Increased 35% as global reinsurers reassessed Florida risk
- New insurer applications: Dropped from 8 in 2006 to 1 in 2007

2008: Senate Bill 2860 - Technical Corrections and Adjustments

Key Changes:

- Allowed limited rate increases for Citizens (max 10% for most policies)
- Created "wind-only" policies to reduce Citizens' exposure
- Established depopulation targets

Outcomes:

- Citizens policy count: Stabilized at 1.1 million
- Private takeouts: 245,000 policies moved to private market
- However: 4 insurers became insolvent during this period

2009: Senate Bill 1950 - The "Glide Path" Introduction

Core Concept: Gradual rate increases rather than market-based pricing

Specifications:

- Annual rate increase cap: 10% for most Citizens policies
- Exception: 15% for vacation homes and secondary residences
- Timeline: No end date specified for reaching actuarial soundness

Five-Year Impact (2009-2014):

- Citizens rates: Increased average 47% (still 23% below actuarial)
- Private market response: 7 new insurers entered market
- But: Coverage restrictions increased (higher deductibles, excluded coverages)

2011: House Bill 1243 - Depopulation Acceleration

Goals: Shrink Citizens by moving policies to private market

Mechanisms:

- Allowed surplus lines insurers to take Citizens policies
- Reduced regulatory requirements for takeout companies
- Created financial incentives for depopulation

Results by 2013:

- Policies moved: 621,000
- New insurers created specifically for takeouts: 12
- Concern: Many undercapitalized (average surplus $18 million vs. $245 million for established carriers)

The Litigation Crisis Period (2012-2021)

2017: House Bill 1421 - Assignment of Benefits Reform Attempt

Problem Addressed: Explosion in water damage claims and litigation

- 2010: 24,671 suits filed
- 2016: 79,234 suits filed (221% increase)

Provisions: Limited attorney fees, required detailed estimates

Effectiveness: Minimal - lawsuits continued climbing

2019: House Bill 7065 - Claims Process Changes[34]

Major Change: Extended hurricane claims deadline from 2 to 3 years

Rationale: Allow homeowners more time to discover hidden damage

Unintended Consequences:

- Reopened claims from 2016-2017 hurricanes: 47,000

- Unable to close books on Hurricane Irma (2017) until 2020
- Litigation on reopened claims: 68% involved attorney representation
- Average claim cost increased: From $19,847 to $43,223 for reopened claims

2021: Senate Bill 76 - Comprehensive Reform Attempt

Key Provisions:

- Reduced time to file claims from 3 years back to 2 years (partially reversing HB 7065)
- Required detailed written notice before filing suits
- Limited attorney fee multipliers

Market Response:

- Litigation: Decreased 15% in first year
- But: 6 insurers still became insolvent 2021-2022
- Premium increases continued: Average 33% in 2021

The Market Stabilization Attempts (2022-2023)

2022: Senate Bill 2-D (May Special Session)[35]

Crisis Trigger:

- Citizens policy count exceeded 1 million
- 6 insurer insolvencies in 18 months[36]
- Average premium increase: 40% year-over-year

Reform Package:

1. **$2 billion Reinsurance Fund** to support private insurers
2. **Litigation reforms**:
    - Eliminated one-way attorney fees
    - Prohibited assignment of benefits for property claims
    - Shortened claim filing deadline to 18 months
3. **Building improvements**: $150 million for home hardening grants

Early Indicators (6 months post-implementation):

- New lawsuits filed: Decreased 35%
- New insurer interest: 3 applications filed
- Citizens growth rate: Slowed from 6,000/week to 3,000/week

2022: Senate Bill 2-A (December Special Session)[37]

Additional Measures:

- Further tightened litigation rules
- Established mandatory binding arbitration for claims under $15,000
- Required detailed inspections for roofs over 15 years old

2023: House Bill 1A - Market Conduct and Rate Flexibility

Focus: Balance rate adequacy with availability

Provisions:

- Allowed expedited rate reviews for qualified insurers
- Increased flexibility for policy forms
- Enhanced market conduct oversight

Status (as of late 2023):

- Citizens policy count: 1.35 million (slight decrease from peak of 1.41 million)
- Private market: Showing signs of stabilization
- New capital: $1.8 billion entered through new insurers and reinsurance facilities

Cumulative Market Impact Summary (2004-2023)

Market Concentration Evolution

- **2004**: 147 insurers writing homeowners coverage
    - Top 10 market share: 52%
    - HHI: 485 (competitive)
- **2023**: 64 insurers actively writing
    - Top 10 market share: 78%
    - HHI: 1,247 (moderately concentrated)
    - Citizens alone: 19% market share

Premium Trajectory

- **2004 average premium**: $1,386
- **2023 average premium**: $4,231
- **Cumulative increase**: 205%
- **National average increase (same period)**: 78%[38]
- **Florida premium as % above national average**:

- 2004: 45% higher
- 2023: 182% higher

Capital Migration

- **Domestic insurers**:
  - 2004 surplus: $8.7 billion
  - 2023 surplus: $4.2 billion
  - Decline: 52%
- **Foreign/Alien insurers**:
  - 2004 market share: 12%
  - 2023 market share: 31%
  - Shift to offshore capital markets

Litigation Metrics

- **2004**: 3,421 suits (0.19% of claims)
- **Peak 2019**: 84,537 suits (8.7% of claims)
- **2023**: 41,232 suits (4.1% of claims)
- **Florida's share of nationwide homeowners litigation**:
  - 2004: 9%
  - 2019: 76%
  - 2023: 48%

Appendix B: Global Case Studies in Policy-Driven Market Uncertainty

Introduction: Patterns Across Markets and Borders

The phenomenon of policy-driven uncertainty destroying market stability is not unique to Florida's insurance crisis. Across the globe, in sectors ranging from healthcare to energy to financial services, the same pattern emerges: well-intentioned government interventions create unpredictability that drives capital flight, reduces competition, and ultimately harms the consumers these policies were meant to protect.

This appendix presents detailed case studies from multiple countries and sectors, providing the quantitative evidence that supports the book's central thesis. Each case study follows a consistent structure: the initial market conditions, the policy interventions, the intended goals, and the actual outcomes measured through specific metrics. By examining these diverse examples through the same analytical lens, we can identify universal principles about how uncertainty affects markets, regardless of geography or industry.

Case Study 1: United States Healthcare - The ACA Exchange Markets (2010-2020)

Market Background

Prior to 2010, the individual health insurance market in the United States served approximately 10.6 million people, with significant variation in coverage, pricing, and availability across states.

Policy Interventions and Timeline

2010 - Patient Protection and Affordable Care Act (ACA)

- Guaranteed issue regardless of pre-existing conditions
- Community rating restrictions (3:1 age bands)
- Essential health benefits mandate
- Individual mandate penalty
- Premium subsidies for 100-400% of federal poverty level

2013-2014 - Implementation Phase

- Risk corridor program (intended to run 2014-2016)
- Reinsurance program ($10 billion in 2014)
- Risk adjustment mechanism

2016 - Risk Corridor Shortfall

- Program collected $362 million but owed $2.87 billion

- Government paid only 12.6% of obligations

2017 - Cost-Sharing Reduction (CSR) Payments Terminated

- $7 billion annual payments ended October 2017
- Insurers required to continue providing benefits

Market Impact Data

Table B.1: ACA Exchange Market Evolution

Year	Participating Insurers	Counties with 1 Insurer	Avg Premium (Age 27)	Claims Ratio
2014	253	7%	$249	92%
2015	237	9%	$256	97%
2016	228	21%	$296	103%
2017	167	33%	$359	99%
2018	132	52%	$411	95%
2019	169	38%	$406	93%
2020	178	29%	$400	91%

Capital Flight Analysis

Major Insurer Exits:

- **UnitedHealth Group**:
    - 2016: Operated in 34 states
    - 2017: Withdrew to 3 states
    - Losses cited: $475 million in 2015, $650 million in 2016
- **Aetna**:
    - 2016: 15 states
    - 2017: 4 states
    - Losses: $430 million (2014-2016 combined)
- **Humana**:
    - 2016: 15 states
    - 2018: Complete exit from exchanges
    - Losses: $54 million in 2016 alone

Table B.2: Market Concentration Changes

Metric	2014	2017	2020
Average insurers per state	5.0	3.5	4.1
HHI (median state)	3,857	5,214	4,892
States with effective monopoly (>50% share)	4	18	12

Uncertainty Drivers

1. **Risk Corridor Failure**: 87.4% shortfall created $2.5 billion uncertainty
2. **CSR Payment Termination**: $7 billion annual funding eliminated without warning
3. **Individual Mandate Repeal** (2019): Core mechanism for risk pooling removed
4. **Regulatory Whiplash**: 47 significant regulatory changes 2014-2020

Outcomes vs. Intentions

Intended: Expand coverage to 32 million uninsured Americans **Actual**: Peak enrollment 12.7 million (2016), declined to 11.4 million (2020)

Intended: Reduce premiums through competition **Actual**: Premiums increased 65% (2014-2018) before stabilizing

Intended: Ensure market competition **Actual**: 52% of counties had only one insurer option by 2018

Case Study 2: Spain's Solar Energy Market Collapse (2007-2013)

Market Background

Spain aimed to become a global leader in renewable energy, with solar photovoltaic (PV) capacity of just 690 MW in 2006.

Policy Interventions

2007 - Royal Decree 661/2007

- Guaranteed feed-in tariff: €0.44/kWh for 25 years
- Annual inflation adjustments
- No capacity limits
- Tariff 10x higher than wholesale electricity prices

2008 - Royal Decree 1578/2008

- Introduced capacity caps (500 MW/year)
- Reduced tariffs by 30%
- Applied to new installations only

2010 - Royal Decree 1565/2010

- Retroactive tariff cuts for existing plants
- Limited guaranteed payment period to 25-28 years
- Reduced rates by additional 45%

2012-2013 - Series of Emergency Decrees

- 7% tax on all electricity generation
- Eliminated inflation adjustments
- Capped reasonable return at 7.5%

Market Impact Data

Table B.3: Spanish Solar Market Evolution

Year	Annual Installations (MW)	Cumulative Capacity (MW)	Investment (€ Billion)	Jobs
2007	544	690	2.1	15,000
2008	2,661	3,351	8.4	41,000
2009	69	3,420	0.2	38,000
2010	420	3,840	1.1	28,000
2011	354	4,194	0.9	19,000
2012	199	4,393	0.5	12,000
2013	120	4,513	0.3	7,500

Financial Impact Analysis

Table B.4: Investment and Returns

Metric	Pre-2010 Promise	Post-2013 Reality	Loss
Project IRR	12-15%	3-5%	-65%
Payback period	7-8 years	15-20 years	+125%
Asset values	€100 baseline	€35-40	-62%
Total stranded investment	-	-	€20 billion

Legal and Reputational Costs

- **International arbitration claims:** 47 cases filed
- **Total claims amount:** €8.3 billion

- **Awards against Spain**: €1.1 billion (as of 2020)
- **Country risk premium increase**: 85 basis points (2011-2013)

Capital Flight Metrics

Foreign Investment in Spanish Renewables:

- 2008: €6.2 billion
- 2009: €0.8 billion
- 2010: €1.1 billion
- 2011: €0.4 billion
- 2012: €0.2 billion
- 2013: €0.1 billion

Decline: 98.4% reduction in 5 years

Case Study 3: United Kingdom Flood Insurance - From Crisis to Flood Re (2000-2020)

Market Background

The UK's "Gentlemen's Agreement" between government and insurers (1961-2000) provided universal flood coverage, but increasing flood events stressed this informal system.

The Crisis Period (2000-2013)

Flood Events and Losses:

- 2000: Autumn floods, £1.3 billion
- 2007: Summer floods, £3.2 billion
- 2012: Widespread flooding, £1.3 billion

Market Response Without Clear Framework:

Table B.5: UK Flood Insurance Market Deterioration

Year	Properties at Risk	Able to Get Coverage	Average Premium	Excess/Deductible
2000	2.3 million	98%	£241	£150
2005	2.4 million	95%	£398	£350
2010	2.7 million	88%	£627	£1,000
2013	2.7 million	79%	£1,042	£2,500

The Flood Re Solution (2013-Present)

Design Principles:

- 25-year transition to risk-reflective pricing
- Capped premiums based on council tax bands
- Industry levy: £180 million annually
- Covers properties built before 2009

Table B.6: Flood Re Performance Metrics

Year	Properties Covered	Claims Paid	Avg Premium	Market Availability
2016	137,000	£12.5m	£296	92%
2017	175,000	£27.3m	£289	95%
2018	212,000	£31.7m	£285	97%
2019	248,000	£64.2m	£283	98%
2020	287,000	£71.4m	£279	99%

Comparative Uncertainty Analysis

Pre-Flood Re Uncertainty Indicators:

- Insurer participation variance: 47% year-to-year
- Premium volatility: 31% annual standard deviation
- Coverage denial rate: Increased 250% (2000-2013)

Post-Flood Re Stability Indicators:

- Insurer participation variance: 3% year-to-year
- Premium volatility: 4% annual standard deviation
- Coverage denial rate: Decreased 85% (2016-2020)

Case Study 4: Germany's Nuclear Energy Phase-Out (2011-2023)

Market Background

Nuclear power provided 23% of Germany's electricity in 2010, with 17 operational reactors and planned lifetime extensions to 2040s.

Policy Shock

March 2011 - Fukushima Disaster May 2011 - Immediate Policy Response:

- 8 reactors shut down immediately
- Remaining 9 to close by 2022
- No compensation initially offered

Market Impact Data

Table B.7: German Electricity Market Transformation

Year	Nuclear Capacity (GW)	Nuclear Share	Wholesale Price (€/MWh)	CO2 Emissions (MT)
2010	20.3	22.2%	44.5	332
2011	12.1	17.6%	51.1	329
2013	12.1	15.4%	37.8	351
2015	10.8	14.1%	31.6	348
2018	9.5	11.7%	44.5	311
2020	8.1	11.3%	30.5	251
2022	4.1	6.0%	235.5	281
2023	0	0%	92.3	295

Stranded Assets and Compensation

Table B.8: Financial Impact on Utilities

Company	Book Value Nuclear Assets 2010	Impairment Charges	Compensation Received	Net Loss
E.ON	€8.2 billion	€6.8 billion	€1.4 billion	€5.4 billion
RWE	€6.7 billion	€5.9 billion	€0.9 billion	€5.0 billion
EnBW	€4.1 billion	€3.5 billion	€0.8 billion	€2.7 billion
Vattenfall	€3.9 billion	€3.2 billion	€1.7 billion	€1.5 billion
Total	€22.9 billion	€19.4 billion	€4.8 billion	€14.6 billion

Broader Economic Effects

Energy-Intensive Industry Impact:

- Aluminum production: -18% (2011-2015)
- Chemical sector energy costs: +31%
- Industrial relocations: 37 major facilities moved abroad

Grid Stability Costs:

- Grid interventions 2010: 290
- Grid interventions 2022: 8,175
- Redispatch costs 2010: €130 million
- Redispatch costs 2022: €4.2 billion

Case Study 5: Japan's Earthquake Insurance Market Evolution (1966-2023)

Market Background

Japan created the world's first government-backed earthquake insurance system in 1966, following the 1964 Niigata earthquake.

System Design and Stability

Original Framework (1966):

- Government-private partnership
- Mandatory offering with fire insurance
- Capped coverage: 30% of fire insurance amount
- Maximum payout: ¥5 trillion

Table B.9: Japanese Earthquake Insurance Evolution

Period	Major Event	Penetration Rate	Claims Paid	System Response
1966-1994	Various	9% → 16%	¥18 billion total	Gradual growth
1995	Kobe Earthquake	16%	¥78.3 billion	Coverage increased to 50%
1996-2010	Stability period	16% → 23%	¥42 billion total	Reserve building
2011	Tohoku Earthquake	23%	¥1.28 trillion	System held, minor adjustments
2012-2023	Recovery	23% → 35%	¥180 billion total	Confidence increased

Stability Through Predictability

Key Design Features:

- Clear coverage limits known in advance
- Transparent reserve requirements
- Gradual, predictable premium adjustments
- No retroactive changes

Table B.10: Comparative Volatility Metrics

Metric	Japan Earthquake	Florida Hurricane	California Earthquake
Premium volatility (std dev)	4.2%	31.7%	8.6%
Insurer entry/exit rate	0.8%	12.4%	3.2%
Coverage availability	99.8%	72-95%	85-92%
Political intervention frequency	0.3/year	2.7/year	0.6/year

Case Study 6: Cyber Insurance Markets - Global Uncertainty (2015-2023)

Market Evolution

The cyber insurance market represents a new frontier where uncertainty dominates due to evolving threats, unclear policy coverage, and inconsistent regulation.

Table B.11: Global Cyber Insurance Market Growth and Volatility

Year	Gross Premiums ($ Billion)	Loss Ratio	Capacity Available	Major Events
2015	2.5	42%	Abundant	Anthem breach
2016	3.1	47%	Abundant	DNC hack
2017	3.8	51%	Growing	WannaCry, NotPetya
2018	5.2	68%	Stable	Multiple breaches
2019	7.1	72%	Tightening	Ransomware surge
2020	9.2	89%	Contracting	SolarWinds
2021	11.9	94%	Severe contraction	Colonial Pipeline
2022	13.8	82%	Stabilizing	War exclusions added
2023	15.4	73%	Selective growth	Regulatory clarity

Regulatory Uncertainty Impact

Table B.12: Regulatory Approaches and Market Response

Jurisdiction	Regulatory Approach	Market Response	Premium Change	Capacity Change
EU (GDPR)	Clear requirements, high penalties	Stable growth	+45%	+30%
USA	Patchwork state/federal	High volatility	+180%	-15%
Singapore	Clear framework	Strong growth	+65%	+75%
China	Restrictive, unclear	Limited market	N/A	-60%

Uncertainty Indicators

Coverage Uncertainty:

- "Silent cyber" exposure: $140-600 billion (estimated range)
- War/terrorism exclusion disputes: 2,847 cases pending
- Systemic event definition: No industry consensus

Pricing Uncertainty:

- Rate-on-line variance: 15-400% for similar risks

- Model divergence: 300%+ difference between vendors
- Historical data: <10 years meaningful data

Synthesis: Universal Patterns

Common Uncertainty Triggers Across All Case Studies

Table B.13: Policy Actions and Market Reactions

Policy Type	Examples	Typical Market Response	Capital Impact
Retroactive changes	Spain solar, Florida claims	Immediate exit	-40% to -80%
Price controls	Florida rates, UK pre-Flood Re	Gradual withdrawal	-20% to -50%
Sudden mandates	Germany nuclear, ACA coverage	Stranded assets	-30% to -70%
Unclear frameworks	US cyber, early ACA	Reduced participation	-25% to -60%
Stable frameworks	Japan earthquake, UK Flood Re	Capital inflow	+15% to +40%

Quantified Uncertainty Costs

Table B.14: Economic Impact of Uncertainty

Market	Direct Costs	Indirect Costs	Total Economic Impact
Florida Insurance	$14.6B capital flight	$28B higher premiums	$42.6 billion
US Healthcare (ACA)	$2.8B insurer losses	$45B reduced access	$47.8 billion
Spain Solar	€20B stranded assets	€15B lost growth	€35 billion
Germany Nuclear	€14.6B write-offs	€31B higher energy costs	€45.6 billion
Global Cyber	$8B capacity reduction	$23B uncovered losses	$31 billion

Recovery Patterns

Markets that successfully reduced uncertainty shared common characteristics:

1. **Clear long-term frameworks** (UK Flood Re, Japan earthquake)
2. **Gradual transitions** (UK's 25-year plan, Japan's stepped coverage)
3. **Stakeholder engagement** (UK consultations, Japan's consensus building)

4. **Predictable adjustments** (Japan's formula-based pricing)
5. **No retroactive changes** (Both UK and Japan honored existing arrangements)

Conclusion

These case studies demonstrate that policy-driven uncertainty is neither sector-specific nor culturally bound. Whether in Florida's insurance market, Spain's solar sector, or Germany's energy system, the pattern is consistent: sudden, unpredictable policy changes drive capital away, concentrate risk, and ultimately harm the constituencies these policies aim to protect. Conversely, markets with stable, predictable frameworks—even those facing severe natural catastrophe risk like Japan—maintain healthy capital flows and broad coverage availability. The lesson is clear: in markets, as in life, it is not the storms we can see coming that destroy us, but the ground that shifts beneath our feet without warning.

Appendix C: Comparative Market Data & Analyses

Introduction: Learning from Parallel Markets

While Florida's insurance crisis provides the most detailed case study, the patterns of policy-driven uncertainty appear across multiple markets and jurisdictions. This appendix presents comparative data that demonstrates how different regulatory approaches yield predictably different outcomes. By examining these parallel experiences, policymakers can better understand which interventions strengthen markets and which destroy them.

Section 1: Interstate Insurance Market Comparisons

1.1 Catastrophe Insurance Markets Across High-Risk States

Table C.1: State Market Health Indicators (2023)

Metric	Florida	California	Texas	Louisiana	South
Market Structure					
Active Insurers	64	112	147	58	89
HHI Score	1,247	892	756	1,389	967
Residual Market Share	19.0%	3.2%	4.8%	22.3%	7.2%
Premium Metrics					
Average Premium	$4,231	$1,428	$2,146	$3,892	$2,234
10-Year Growth	205%	42%	67%	187%	98%
Volatility (Std Dev)	31.7%	8.6%	12.3%	28.4%	15.6%
Risk Transfer					
Reinsurance	27%	15%	18%	25%	20%
Cat Bond Usage	High	Medium	Low	Medium	Low
Legal Environment					
Litigation Rate	10.6%	1.2%	2.3%	7.8%	3.4%
Avg Legal Cost/Claim	$9,234	$2,156	$3,421	$7,892	$4,123
Capital Metrics					
5-Year Capital Change	-18%	+12%	+8%	-14%	+3%
New Entrants (5yr)	15	23	31	8	19
Exits (5yr)	34	11	17	19	14

Key Observations:

- States with stable regulatory frameworks (California, Texas) show lower HHI scores, premium volatility, and positive capital flows
- Florida and Louisiana, with frequent legislative interventions, show the highest residual market shares and capital flight
- Litigation rates correlate strongly (r=0.89) with premium volatility

1.2 Regulatory Approach Comparison

Table C.2: Policy Stability Index by State

State	Major Legislative Changes (2013-2023)	Average Implementation Period	Retroactive Changes	Stability Score (0-100)
California	3	18 months	0	82
Texas	5	12 months	1	74
South Carolina	7	9 months	1	61
Louisiana	11	6 months	3	43
Florida	14	4 months	4	31

Correlation Analysis:

- Stability Score vs. Market HHI: r = -0.84 (higher stability = lower concentration)
- Stability Score vs. Premium Growth: r = -0.91 (higher stability = lower premium growth)
- Stability Score vs. Capital Inflow: r = 0.87 (higher stability = more capital)

Section 2: Cross-Sector Uncertainty Analysis

2.1 Healthcare Markets: ACA Implementation Variations

Table C.3: State Healthcare Exchange Performance (2014-2020)

State	Regulatory Consistency	Insurer Participation Change	Premium Volatility	Current Market Status
Stable Frameworks				
Massachusetts	Consistent support	+4 insurers	8.2%	11 insurers, competitive
Connecticut	Steady implementation	+2 insurers	11.3%	7 insurers, stable
Rhode Island	Minimal changes	+1 insurer	9.7%	5 insurers, stable
Volatile Frameworks				
Iowa	Multiple reversals	-6 insurers	34.2%	2 insurers, concentrated
Tennessee	Conflicting policies	-8 insurers	41.3%	3 insurers, bare counties
Arizona	Uncertain subsidies	-9 insurers	38.6%	4 insurers, limited options

Impact Metrics:

- Stable states: Average premium increase 2014-2020: 38%
- Volatile states: Average premium increase 2014-2020: 127%
- Consumer access: 94% coverage in stable states vs. 71% in volatile states

2.2 Energy Market Policy Comparisons

Table C.4: Renewable Energy Policy Outcomes by Country

Country	Policy Approach	Investment Stability	Market Outcome	Capital Impact
Consistent Policies				
Denmark	30-year consistent support	Very High	Global wind leader	+€45B investment
Japan	Feed-in tariff maintained	High	9% solar penetration	+¥12T investment
UK	Clear transition timelines	High	42% renewable by 2023	+£198B investment
Inconsistent Policies				
Spain	Retroactive subsidy cuts	Collapsed	96% investment drop	-€20B stranded
Czech Republic	Sudden FIT termination	Very Low	80% market exit	-€3B losses
Poland	Policy reversals	Low	<15% renewable	-€8B foregone

Section 3: Market Recovery Patterns

3.1 Post-Crisis Recovery Velocity Comparison

Table C.5: Recovery Speed After Major Market Disruptions

Event	Initial Capacity Loss	Policy Response	Recovery Time	Full Recovery?
Predictable Responses				
Japan Earthquake 2011	-23%	Maintained framework	18 months	Yes
UK Floods 2007	-31%	Created Flood Re	24 months	Yes
NZ Earthquake 2011	-28%	Public-private partnership	30 months	Yes
Unpredictable Responses				
Florida 2004-05	-41%	Multiple interventions	18+ years	No
Louisiana Katrina	-38%	Regulatory chaos	12+ years	Partial
Australia Cyclone 2011	-19%	Price controls	8 years	Yes

Recovery Velocity Formula Applied:

- Predictable policy markets: Average 14.2% capacity recovery per year
- Unpredictable policy markets: Average 4.3% capacity recovery per year

3.2 Capital Flow Patterns

Table C.6: Capital Response to Policy Announcements

Policy Type	First Month Response	Six Month Response	One Year Response	Permanent Impact
Positive Certainty Signals				
Clear long-term framework	+2-3%	+8-12%	+15-20%	+25-30%
Reduced litigation rules	+1-2%	+5-8%	+10-15%	+15-20%
Market-based pricing	+3-4%	+10-15%	+18-25%	+30-40%
Negative Uncertainty Signals				
Rate freeze/cap	-5-8%	-15-20%	-25-35%	-40-50%
Retroactive changes	-8-12%	-20-30%	-35-45%	-50-60%
Coverage mandates	-3-5%	-10-15%	-20-25%	-25-35%

Section 4: Cost-Benefit Analysis of Regulatory Approaches

4.1 Economic Impact Comparison

Table C.7: Total Economic Cost of Different Regulatory Approaches

Market/Approach	Direct Costs	Indirect Costs	Total Impact	Per Capita Cost
Florida (Reactive)	$34.2B premiums	$83.1B opportunity	$117.3B (20yr)	$5,442
California (Stable)	$18.7B premiums	$12.3B opportunity	$31.0B (20yr)	$785
Louisiana (Volatile)	$14.3B premiums	$31.2B opportunity	$45.5B (20yr)	$9,782
Texas (Moderate)	$22.1B premiums	$19.8B opportunity	$41.9B (20yr)	$1,445

Components of Indirect Costs:

- Lost economic development from high insurance costs
- Reduced property values in high-premium areas
- Foregone investment due to uncertainty
- State backstop liability exposure

4.2 Consumer Impact Metrics

Table C.8: Consumer Outcomes by Regulatory Approach

Metric	Stable Regulation	Moderate Regulation	Volatile Regulation
Coverage Availability	95-99%	85-95%	70-85%
Average Wait for Quote	1-2 days	3-5 days	7-14 days
Policy Options	8-12	4-8	1-3
Non-renewal Risk	<5%	5-10%	10-25%
Premium Predictability	±10%	±20%	±40%
Claims Satisfaction	82%	71%	54%

Section 5: International Best Practices

5.1 Successful Market Stabilization Programs

Table C.9: Elements of Successful Programs

Program	Key Features	Uncertainty	Market Result
Japan Earthquake	60-year consistent framework,	-76%	99.8% availability
UK Flood Re	25-year transition plan, clear	-71%	95% → 99%
California CEA	Risk-based pricing, public-private	-64%	Stable since 1996
Swiss Natural Hazard	Mandatory but private, consistent	-79%	100% coverage
French Cat Nat	Uniform add-on premium, state	-69%	Universal

Common Success Factors:

1. Long-term framework (minimum 10 years)
2. Clear, published transition plans
3. No retroactive changes
4. Stakeholder involvement in design
5. Regular but predictable adjustments

5.2 Failed Interventions

Table C.10: Common Features of Failed Programs

Intervention Type	Example Markets	Failure Rate	Average Capital Flight
Price freezes without subsidy	FL, LA, MA (auto)	87%	-35%
Retroactive coverage changes	Spain solar, FL claims	92%	-45%
Sudden mandate implementation	ACA early years	76%	-28%
Discretionary rate approval	Several US states	68%	-22%
Politically driven changes	Multiple markets	83%	-38%

Section 6: Predictive Indicators

6.1 Early Warning Signals Across Markets

Table C.11: Universal Warning Signs of Market Stress

Indicator	Green Zone	Yellow Zone	Red Zone	Time to Crisis
Regulatory changes/year	<2	2-4	>4	18-24 months
Capital flow trend	Positive	Flat	Negative	12-18 months
Market concentration Δ	<50 HHI/yr	50-100	>100	24-36 months
Premium volatility	<10%	10-20%	>20%	12-24 months
New entrant ratio	>1.5	0.8-1.5	<0.8	18-30 months

6.2 Recovery Indicators

Table C.12: Signs of Market Stabilization

Recovery Signal	Measurement	Threshold	Typical Timeline
Capital return	Quarterly inflow	>$100M	Months 3-6
New entrants	Applications filed	>2	Months 6-12
Premium stabilization	Volatility decrease	<15%	Months 12-18
Litigation decline	Case reduction	>20%	Months 6-9
Reinsurance costs	Rate decrease	>10%	Months 12-24

Conclusions from Comparative Analysis

The comparative data reveals consistent patterns:

1. **Regulatory Stability = Market Health**: Every 1-point increase in stability score correlates with 2.3% lower premiums and 15% more capital
2. **Speed Kills**: Implementation periods under 6 months show 3x higher failure rates
3. **Retroactivity Is Toxic**: Any retroactive change correlates with minimum 25% capital flight
4. **Recovery Takes Time**: Markets need 3-5x longer to recover than to collapse
5. **Litigation Is Contagious**: High litigation states infect neighboring markets through reinsurer repricing

These patterns hold across insurance, healthcare, and energy markets, across countries and cultures, suggesting fundamental economic principles at work rather than sector-specific phenomena.

Appendix D1: Quantifying Uncertainty - A Comprehensive Methodology

Introduction: Measuring the Unmeasurable

While uncertainty by definition resists precise quantification, several metrics can serve as proxies to gauge the level of uncertainty in catastrophe insurance markets. This appendix provides detailed methodologies for measuring market uncertainty, complete with calculations, interpretations, and practical applications.

Core Metrics for Uncertainty Assessment

1. Insurance Penetration Rate (IPR)

Definition: The percentage of eligible properties carrying catastrophe insurance in high-risk areas.

Formula:

IPR = (Number of Insured Properties / Total Eligible Properties) × 100

Data Requirements:

- Census of residential properties in designated high-risk zones
- Active insurance policies by zip code
- Adjustment for mortgage requirements vs. voluntary purchase

Measurement Methodology:

1. Define high-risk zones using FEMA flood maps and state windpool territories
2. Obtain property counts from tax assessor databases
3. Match with insurance policy databases (admitted and surplus lines)
4. Calculate quarterly to capture seasonal variations

Florida Case Study Application:

- **2010 Baseline**:
    - Coastal counties properties: 2,847,000
    - Insured properties: 2,220,660
    - IPR: 78.0%

- **2020 Measurement**:
  - Coastal counties properties: 3,156,000
  - Insured properties: 2,272,320
  - IPR: 72.0%
- **Interpretation**: 6 percentage point decline indicates 190,000+ properties moved to self-insurance or no insurance, suggesting reduced market confidence

Uncertainty Signal Thresholds:

- IPR > 85%: Low uncertainty (healthy market)
- IPR 70-85%: Moderate uncertainty (monitoring needed)
- IPR < 70%: High uncertainty (market stress)

2. Premium-to-Coverage Ratio (PCR)

Definition: The cost per $1,000 of coverage, adjusted for inflation and underlying risk changes.

Formula:

PCR = (Annual Premium / Coverage Amount) × 1,000

Adjusted PCR = PCR / (Inflation Index × Risk Index)

Risk Index Calculation:

- Base year = 100
- Adjust for: Updated hurricane models, building code changes, population density shifts
- Example: If hurricane risk increased 15% due to climate factors, Risk Index = 115

Florida Detailed Calculations:

2005 Baseline:

- Average premium: $1,847
- Average coverage: $437,000
- Raw PCR: $4.23 per $1,000
- Inflation adjustment: 1.00 (base year)
- Risk adjustment: 1.00 (base year)

- Adjusted PCR: $4.23

2020 Analysis:

- Average premium: $3,926
- Average coverage: $512,000
- Raw PCR: $7.67 per $1,000
- Inflation adjustment: 1.31 (31% cumulative inflation)
- Risk adjustment: 1.18 (18% increase in modeled hurricane risk)
- Adjusted PCR: $7.67 / (1.31 × 1.18) = $4.96

Interpretation:

- Real increase: $0.73 per $1,000 (17.3% above risk-adjusted baseline)
- This excess represents the "uncertainty premium" charged by insurers

3. Market Concentration Index (Herfindahl-Hirschman Index)

Definition: Sum of squared market shares, measuring competitive dynamics.

Formula:

$$HHI = \Sigma(\text{Market Share\_i})^2 \times 10{,}000$$

Calculation Steps:

1. Obtain premium volume for each insurer
2. Calculate market share percentages
3. Square each share and sum
4. Multiply by 10,000 for standard scale

Florida Market Evolution:

2005 Calculation:

- Top 5 insurers: 15%, 12%, 10%, 8%, 7% = 52% combined
- Next 15 insurers: Average 2.4% each = 36% combined
- Remaining 127 insurers: 12% combined

- $HHI = 15^2 + 12^2 + 10^2 + 8^2 + 7^2 + (15 \times 2.4^2)$ + small firm approximation
- HHI = 225 + 144 + 100 + 64 + 49 + 86 + 12 = 680

2020 Calculation:

- Citizens: 18%
- Top 4 private: 14%, 11%, 9%, 8% = 42% combined
- Next 10: Average 3% each = 30% combined
- Remaining 49: 10% combined
- $HHI = 18^2 + 14^2 + 11^2 + 9^2 + 8^2 + (10 \times 3^2)$ + small firm approximation
- HHI = 324 + 196 + 121 + 81 + 64 + 90 + 10 = 886

2023 Calculation:

- Citizens: 19%
- Top 4 private: 16%, 13%, 10%, 9% = 48% combined
- Next 8: Average 3.5% each = 28% combined
- Remaining 51: 5% combined
- $HHI = 361 + 256 + 169 + 100 + 81 + (8 \times 3.5^2) + 5 = 1,247$

Market Concentration Classifications:

- HHI < 1,000: Unconcentrated (healthy competition)
- HHI 1,000-1,800: Moderately concentrated
- HHI > 1,800: Highly concentrated (competition concerns)

4. Reinsurance Cost Index (RCI)

Definition: The cost of reinsurance as a percentage of primary premium, compared to baseline.

Formula:

RCI = (Reinsurance Cost / Gross Premium Written) × 100

Relative RCI = Current RCI / Baseline RCI

Data Collection Method:

- Quarterly statutory filings (Schedule F)
- Separate traditional reinsurance from alternative capital
- Include both proportional and non-proportional treaties

Florida Analysis:

2005 Baseline:

- Gross premiums: $14.7 billion
- Reinsurance cost: $1.47 billion
- RCI: 10.0%

2010 (Post-crisis):

- Gross premiums: $11.2 billion
- Reinsurance cost: $2.24 billion
- RCI: 20.0%
- Relative RCI: 2.00 (100% increase)

2020:

- Gross premiums: $18.3 billion
- Reinsurance cost: $4.58 billion
- RCI: 25.0%
- Relative RCI: 2.50 (150% increase from baseline)

Component Analysis:

- Traditional reinsurance: 60% of total, priced at 3.2x baseline
- Catastrophe bonds: 25% of total, priced at 1.8x baseline
- Collateralized reinsurance: 15% of total, priced at 2.1x baseline

5. Litigation Intensity Ratio (LIR)

Definition: Frequency and cost of insurance-related litigation relative to claims.

Two-Part Formula:

Frequency LIR = (Lawsuits Filed / Total Claims) × 100

Cost LIR = (Legal Costs / Total Claims Paid) × 100

Combined LIR = (Frequency LIR × 0.5) + (Cost LIR × 0.5)

Florida Detailed Tracking:

2015 Baseline:

- Claims filed: 287,432
- Lawsuits filed: 14,372
- Frequency LIR: 5.0%
- Total claims paid: $3.2 billion
- Legal costs: $128 million
- Cost LIR: 4.0%
- Combined LIR: 4.5%

2019 Peak Crisis:

- Claims filed: 412,837
- Lawsuits filed: 71,830
- Frequency LIR: 17.4%
- Total claims paid: $5.8 billion
- Legal costs: $1.16 billion
- Cost LIR: 20.0%
- Combined LIR: 18.7%

2023 Post-Reform:

- Claims filed: 389,421
- Lawsuits filed: 31,154

- Frequency LIR: 8.0%
- Total claims paid: $4.9 billion
- Legal costs: $392 million
- Cost LIR: 8.0%
- Combined LIR: 8.0%

6. Capital Adequacy Stress Index (CASI)

Definition: Measures insurer financial strength under stress scenarios.

Formula:

CASI = (Available Capital - Stress Scenario Loss) / Minimum Required Capital

Stress Scenario Definition:

- 1-in-100 year hurricane event
- Plus 20% adverse development
- Plus litigation costs at 90th percentile

Industry Aggregate Example:

2010:

- Available capital: $8.7 billion
- Stress loss: $14.2 billion
- Minimum required: $4.5 billion
- CASI: (8.7 - 14.2) / 4.5 = -1.22 (severe undercapitalization)

2023:

- Available capital: $6.8 billion
- Stress loss: $11.3 billion
- Minimum required: $4.8 billion
- CASI: (6.8 - 11.3) / 4.8 = -0.94 (improving but still negative)

7. Market Recovery Velocity (MRV)

Definition: Speed at which market capacity returns following a major event.

Formula:

MRV = (Capacity at Time T - Capacity at Event) / (Pre-Event Capacity × T)

Where T = Years since event

Comparative Analysis:

Hurricane Andrew (1992):

- Pre-event capacity: $12 billion
- Post-event capacity: $7 billion
- Recovery to pre-event levels: 4 years
- MRV: (12 - 7) / (12 × 4) = 0.104 (10.4% per year)

2004-2005 Hurricane Seasons:

- Pre-event capacity: $22 billion
- Post-event capacity: $13 billion
- Recovery to pre-event levels: 7 years
- MRV: (22 - 13) / (22 × 7) = 0.058 (5.8% per year)

Interpretation: Slower recovery velocity indicates increased uncertainty

Composite Uncertainty Score (CUS)

Purpose: Combine all metrics into single indicator

Weighted Formula:

CUS = (IPR × 0.15) + (PCR × 0.20) + (HHI × 0.15) +

(RCI × 0.20) + (LIR × 0.15) + (CASI × 0.10) + (MRV × 0.05)

Each metric normalized to 0-100 scale where 100 = maximum uncertainty

Florida Market Composite Scores:

2005: CUS = 28 (Low uncertainty) **2010**: CUS = 67 (High uncertainty) **2015**: CUS = 54 (Moderate uncertainty) **2019**: CUS = 78 (Very high uncertainty) **2023**: CUS = 45 (Moderate uncertainty, improving)

Application Guidelines for Policymakers

Using Metrics for Decision-Making

1. **Baseline Establishment**: Set metrics during stable period as reference
2. **Regular Monitoring**: Track monthly/quarterly, not just annually
3. **Threshold Triggers**: Define automatic review if metrics exceed bounds
4. **Multi-Metric Validation**: Never rely on single indicator
5. **Forward-Looking Adjustments**: Account for known future changes

Red Flag Combinations

Critical Warning Signs (requiring immediate intervention):

- IPR drops >10% in 12 months
- PCR increases >25% above risk-adjusted baseline
- HHI increases >300 points in 24 months
- LIR exceeds 15% for 2 consecutive quarters
- CASI remains negative for 4 quarters

Policy Impact Assessment Template

For any proposed policy, estimate impact on each metric:

- Negligible (0-5% change)
- Minor (5-15% change)
- Moderate (15-30% change)
- Major (>30% change)

Sum weighted impacts to predict total uncertainty effect.

Conclusion

These quantification methods transform the abstract concept of uncertainty into measurable, trackable metrics. While no single measure captures all dimensions of uncertainty, the composite approach provides policymakers with an evidence-based framework for understanding market dynamics and anticipating the consequences of regulatory decisions.

Appendix D2: The Risk-Uncertainty Spectrum Toolkit - Assessment Frameworks for Policymakers

Introduction: From Concept to Application

The Risk-Uncertainty Spectrum introduced in Chapter 2 provides a conceptual framework for understanding how policy decisions affect market stability. This appendix transforms that concept into practical tools that policymakers, regulators, and market participants can use to assess, predict, and monitor the impact of regulatory decisions on capital markets.

This toolkit includes scoring rubrics, decision trees, assessment templates, and monitoring dashboards that enable users to:

- Evaluate proposed policies before implementation
- Track market position on the spectrum in real-time
- Identify early warning signals of increasing uncertainty
- Compare alternative policy approaches objectively
- Build consensus among stakeholders through transparent metrics

Each tool has been calibrated using the real-world data from Florida's insurance market and the global case studies presented in previous appendices.

Tool 1: Policy Impact Assessment Matrix (PIAM)

Purpose

Evaluate proposed policies across multiple dimensions to predict their likely effect on market uncertainty.

Assessment Framework

Table D.1: Policy Impact Scoring Rubric

Dimension	-2 (High Uncertainty)	-1 (Moderate Uncertainty)	0 (Neutral)	+1 (Moderate Certainty)	+2 (High Certainty)
Implementation Timeline	Immediate (<30 days)	Rapid (30-90 days)	Standard (90-180 days)	Gradual (180-365 days)	Phased (>365 days)
Retroactivity	Fully retroactive	Partially retroactive	Current period only	Future only with notice	Future with transition
Price Flexibility	Fixed/frozen prices	Capped increases <5%	Limited bands 5-10%	Guided flexibility 10-20%	Market-based
Stakeholder Input	No consultation	Limited/selective	Standard comment period	Extended consultation	Collaborative design
Predictability	Discretionary changes	Annual reviews	Formula-based	Locked for 3+ years	Constitutional/treaty
Scope	Entire market	>50% of market	25-50% of market	<25% of market	Pilot/voluntary
Complexity	Requires system overhaul	Major process changes	Moderate adjustments	Minor modifications	Clarifications only
Enforcement	Criminal penalties	Civil penalties + litigation	Civil penalties only	Market incentives	Voluntary compliance
Exit Options	No exit permitted	Penalized exit	Delayed exit	Standard exit	Enhanced portability
Data Requirements	New undefined metrics	New defined metrics	Enhanced reporting	Current reporting	Reduced reporting

Scoring Methodology

1. Score each dimension from -2 to +2
2. Apply weights based on market context (see Table D.2)
3. Calculate weighted total
4. Convert to spectrum position

Table D.2: Dimension Weights by Market Type

Dimension	Catastrophe Insurance	Healthcare	Energy	Financial
Implementation Timeline	15%	10%	10%	20%
Retroactivity	20%	15%	20%	15%
Price Flexibility	20%	20%	15%	10%
Stakeholder Input	10%	10%	10%	10%
Predictability	15%	15%	20%	20%
Scope	5%	10%	10%	10%
Complexity	5%	10%	5%	5%
Enforcement	5%	5%	5%	5%
Exit Options	5%	5%	5%	5%
Data Requirements	0%	0%	0%	0%

Interpretation Scale

Total Weighted Score → Spectrum Position:

- +15 to +20: Deep green (high certainty)
- +10 to +14: Green (moderate certainty)
- +5 to +9: Light green (mild certainty)
- -4 to +4: Yellow (neutral)
- -9 to -5: Light red (mild uncertainty)
- -14 to -10: Red (moderate uncertainty)
- -20 to -15: Deep red (high uncertainty)

Example Application: Florida's 2007 Rate Freeze

Dimension	Score	Weight	Weighted
Implementation Timeline	-2	15%	-0.30
Retroactivity	-1	20%	-0.20
Price Flexibility	-2	20%	-0.40
Stakeholder Input	-1	10%	-0.10
Predictability	-2	15%	-0.30
Scope	-2	5%	-0.10
Complexity	-1	5%	-0.05
Enforcement	-1	5%	-0.05
Exit Options	-1	5%	-0.05
Total			**-1.55**

Normalized Score: -1.55 × 10 = -15.5 (Deep red/high uncertainty) **Actual Outcome**: 18% capital flight within 24 months - confirms prediction

---

Tool 2: Market Stability Dashboard

Purpose

Real-time monitoring system to track market position on the Risk-Uncertainty Spectrum.

Core Indicators

Table D.3: Dashboard Metrics and Thresholds

Indicator	Green Zone	Yellow Zone	Red Zone	Data Source	Update Frequency
Capital Flows					
New entrants	>3/year	1-3/year	0/year	Regulatory filings	Quarterly
Exits/withdrawals	<2/year	2-5/year	>5/year	Regulatory filings	Quarterly
Capital injections	>$500M/qtr	$100-500M	<$100M	Financial statements	Quarterly
Market Concentration					
HHI Index	<1000	1000-1800	>1800	Premium data	Annual
Top 5 share	<60%	60-75%	>75%	Market reports	Annual
State entity share	<10%	10-25%	>25%	Regulatory data	Quarterly
Pricing Dynamics					
Rate filing variance	<15%	15-30%	>30%	Rate filings	Monthly
Approval time	<60 days	60-120 days	>120 days	Regulatory data	Monthly
Rate adequacy	95-105%	85-95%	<85%	Actuarial analysis	Quarterly
Consumer Access					
Coverage availability	>95%	85-95%	<85%	Market surveys	Annual
Average quotes/app	>5	3-5	<3	Consumer data	Quarterly
Non-renewal rate	<5%	5-10%	>10%	Company reports	Annual
Legal Environment					
Litigation ratio	<2%	2-5%	>5%	Court records	Quarterly
Avg settlement	<$50K	$50-100K	>$100K	Claims data	Annual
Time to close	<180 days	180-365	>365 days	Claims data	Quarterly

Composite Stability Score

Formula:

Stability Score = Σ(Indicator Score × Weight) / Σ(Weights)

Where each indicator is scored:

- Green = 100
- Yellow = 50
- Red = 0

Early Warning System

Table D.4: Warning Triggers and Required Actions

Warning Level	Trigger Conditions	Required Actions	Timeline
Watch	2+ indicators yellow	Enhanced monitoring	Immediate
Alert	3+ indicators yellow OR 1 red	Stakeholder consultation	30 days
Warning	2+ indicators red	Policy review	60 days
Crisis	3+ indicators red	Emergency intervention	Immediate

Tool 3: Policy Decision Tree Framework

Purpose

Guide policymakers through systematic evaluation of regulatory options.

Decision Tree Structure

```
START: Policy Need Identified
│
├─Q1: Is intervention necessary?
│  ├─NO → Document rationale → END
│  └─YES → Continue
│
├─Q2: What is the primary goal?
│  ├─Consumer protection
│  ├─Market stability
│  ├─Capacity expansion
│  └─Cost reduction
│
├─Q3: What is the risk tolerance?
│  ├─LOW → Gradual approach required
│  ├─MEDIUM → Standard approach
│  └─HIGH → Rapid intervention possible
│
├─Q4: Market concentration level?
│  ├─LOW (<1000 HHI) → More flexibility
│  ├─MEDIUM (1000-1800) → Balanced approach
│  └─HIGH (>1800) → Extreme caution
│
├─Q5: Implementation timeline available?
│  ├─<6 months → Limited options
│  ├─6-12 months → Standard options
│  └─>12 months → Full flexibility
│
└─RECOMMENDATION: [Based on path]
```

Decision Path Scoring

Table D.5: Path Recommendations by Score

Path Score	Recommended Approach	Example Interventions	Risk Level
8-10	Market-based incentives	Tax credits, voluntary programs	Low
6-7	Guided market solutions	Corridors, soft caps	Low-Medium
4-5	Regulatory adjustments	Reporting changes, guidelines	Medium
2-3	Direct intervention	Mandates, requirements	Medium-High
0-1	Emergency measures	Freezes, moratoria	High

Tool 4: Stakeholder Impact Analysis Template

Purpose

Evaluate how different stakeholder groups will be affected by policy changes.

Stakeholder Matrix

Table D.6: Multi-Stakeholder Impact Assessment

Stakeholder	Short-term Impact (0-	Medium-term (1-3	Long-term (3+	Uncertainty
Consumers				
Benefit				
Cost				
Net Impact				Low/Medium/High
Domestic				
Benefit				
Cost				
Net Impact				Low/Medium/High
Reinsurers				
Benefit				
Cost				
Net Impact				Low/Medium/High
Capital Markets				
Benefit				
Cost				
Net Impact				Low/Medium/High
Government				
Benefit				
Cost				
Net Impact				Low/Medium/High

Stakeholder Alignment Score

Calculate alignment by comparing net impacts:

- Aligned: All positive or all negative = Low uncertainty
- Mixed: Some positive, some negative = Medium uncertainty
- Opposed: Strong positive vs. strong negative = High uncertainty

---

Tool 5: Comparative Policy Analyzer

Purpose

Compare multiple policy options using consistent criteria.

Comparison Framework

Table D.7: Policy Option Comparison Template

Criteria	Option A	Option B	Option C	Status Quo
Effectiveness (0-10)				
Achieves stated goal				
Timeline to impact				
Sustainability				
Uncertainty Impact (-10 to +10)				
Predictability				
Flexibility				
Reversibility				
Cost-Benefit				
Direct costs				
Indirect costs				
Benefits				
Implementation (0-10)				
Complexity				
Resources required				
Stakeholder acceptance				
Risk Assessment				
Unintended consequences				
Legal challenges				
Market disruption				
TOTAL SCORE				

Scoring Weights

- Effectiveness: 30%
- Uncertainty Impact: 30%
- Cost-Benefit: 20%
- Implementation: 10%
- Risk Assessment: 10%

Tool 6: Regulatory Intervention Sequencing Guide

Purpose

Determine optimal order and timing for multiple interventions.

Sequencing Principles

Table D.8: Intervention Sequencing Matrix

Intervention Type	Prerequisites	Optimal Timing	Warning Signs	Success Metrics
Information/Transparency	None	Immediate	None	Data quality improvement
Incentives/Subsidies	Baseline data	3-6 months	Budget availability	Uptake rates
Guidelines/Standards	Stakeholder input	6-12 months	Compliance capacity	Adoption rates
Regulatory Requirements	Impact analysis	12-18 months	Market capacity	Compliance rates
Price Controls	All above failed	18-24 months	Market failure	Price stability
Direct Market Entry	Total failure	Last resort	Capital flight	Market stabilization

Sequencing Decision Framework

1. Start with least intrusive (information)
2. Allow time for market response (minimum 6 months)
3. Measure impact before escalating
4. Build on success rather than abandoning
5. Preserve optionality for future adjustments

Tool 7: Cross-Border Regulatory Comparison Tool

Purpose

Learn from international experiences by comparing regulatory approaches.

Comparison Framework

Table D.9: International Regulatory Comparison

Country/Region	Regulatory Approach	Market Outcome	Uncertainty Level	Key Lessons
Catastrophe Insurance				
Florida	Reactive controls	Capital flight	High	Avoid retroactive changes
California	Public-private partnership	Stable	Low	Clear frameworks work
Japan	Long-term planning	Resilient	Very Low	Predictability crucial
Healthcare				
USA (ACA)	Complex mandates	Volatile	High	Simplicity matters
UK (NHS)	Single payer	Stable funding issues	Medium	Political consensus needed
Germany	Social insurance	Stable	Low	Multi-stakeholder governance
Energy				
Spain	Subsidy reversal	Market collapse	Very High	Honor commitments
Germany	Planned transition	Expensive but stable	Medium	Clear timelines help
Denmark	Consistent support	Global leader	Low	Long-term commitment

Tool 8: Dynamic Monitoring and Response Protocol

Purpose

Establish systematic process for ongoing market monitoring and intervention.

Monitoring Protocol

Phase 1: Continuous Monitoring

- Dashboard metrics updated per schedule
- Automated alerts for threshold breaches
- Monthly trend analysis

Phase 2: Trigger Evaluation

- Alert triggers review within 48 hours
- Determine if pattern or anomaly
- Stakeholder notification if pattern

Phase 3: Response Development

- Convene response team
- Apply assessment tools
- Develop options within 30 days

Phase 4: Implementation

- Select least intrusive effective option
- Communicate clearly with market
- Set success metrics and timeline

Phase 5: Evaluation

- Measure against success metrics
- Adjust if necessary
- Document lessons learned

Response Escalation Ladder

Table D.10: Intervention Escalation Protocol

Level	Market Condition	Intervention Type	Authority Required	Review Period
0	Stable	None	None	Annual
1	Watch	Enhanced monitoring	Staff level	Quarterly
2	Concern	Information campaign	Department head	Monthly
3	Alert	Voluntary measures	Commissioner	Bi-weekly
4	Warning	Regulatory guidance	Commissioner	Weekly
5	Critical	Requirements	Legislative	Daily
6	Crisis	Emergency powers	Governor/Minister	Continuous

Tool 9: Success Metrics and Evaluation Framework

Purpose

Define and measure success of regulatory interventions.

Success Metrics by Goal Type

Table D.11: Goal-Specific Success Metrics

Primary Goal	6-Month Metrics	12-Month Metrics	24-Month Metrics	Failure Indicators
Expand Coverage				
	+5% penetration	+10% penetration	+15% penetration	Decreasing availability
	New entrants >2	Sustained capacity	Market growth	Exits exceed entries
Reduce Costs				
	Premium stability	0-5% increase	Below inflation	>10% increase
	Claims efficiency +10%	+20% efficiency	Sustained	Litigation increase
Increase Competition				
	HHI decrease 50+	HHI decrease 100+	HHI <1500	HHI increase
	New products launched	Market share shifts	Innovation	Homogenization
Improve Stability				
	Volatility decrease 20%	Capital inflow	Rating upgrades	Capital flight
	No insolvencies	Profitability	Growth	Losses/exits

Tool 10: Regulatory Sandbox Framework

Purpose

Test new approaches in controlled environment before full implementation.

Sandbox Design Parameters

Table D.12: Sandbox Configuration Options

Parameter	Option A: Conservative	Option B: Moderate	Option C: Aggressive
Scope	Single county/region	Multiple regions	Statewide
Duration	12 months	24 months	36 months
Participants	2-3 volunteers	5-10 selected	Open participation
Products	Single product type	Limited range	Full range
Oversight	Daily reporting	Weekly reporting	Monthly reporting
Exit Rights	Anytime with notice	Quarterly windows	Annual only
Success Criteria	Multiple metrics	Primary metric	Market-based
Rollout Decision	Unanimous approval	Majority approval	Automatic unless stopped

Sandbox Evaluation Matrix

Score each dimension 1-5:

1. Learning value
2. Risk containment
3. Scalability
4. Stakeholder support
5. Resource efficiency

Total Score Interpretation:

- 20-25: Proceed immediately
- 15-19: Proceed with modifications
- 10-14: Reconsider design
- <10: Do not proceed

Implementation Guide: Putting the Tools to Work

Step-by-Step Process for Policy Development

Step 1: Baseline Assessment

- Use Market Stability Dashboard (Tool 2)
- Document current spectrum position
- Identify problem to solve

Step 2: Option Development

- Apply Policy Decision Tree (Tool 3)
- Generate 3-5 options
- Include "do nothing" option

Step 3: Impact Analysis

- Score with Policy Impact Assessment Matrix (Tool 1)
- Complete Stakeholder Impact Analysis (Tool 4)
- Use Comparative Policy Analyzer (Tool 5)

Step 4: Sequencing and Design

- Apply Regulatory Intervention Sequencing Guide (Tool 6)
- Consider Cross-Border Comparisons (Tool 7)
- Design monitoring protocol (Tool 8)

Step 5: Testing (if appropriate)

- Design Regulatory Sandbox (Tool 10)
- Run pilot program
- Evaluate results

Step 6: Implementation

- Execute with clear communication
- Monitor using Dashboard (Tool 2)
- Apply Dynamic Response Protocol (Tool 8)

Step 7: Evaluation

- Measure against Success Metrics (Tool 9)
- Document lessons learned
- Adjust as necessary

Conclusion: From Uncertainty to Understanding

These tools transform the abstract concept of the Risk-Uncertainty Spectrum into actionable frameworks for policy development and market management. By applying these systematic approaches, policymakers can:

1. **Predict** the likely impact of interventions before implementation
2. **Monitor** market conditions in real-time
3. **Respond** appropriately to changing conditions
4. **Learn** from both successes and failures
5. **Build** more resilient markets over time

The Florida insurance crisis and global case studies demonstrate the devastating cost of policy uncertainty. These tools offer a path toward more thoughtful, effective regulation that maintains market stability while achieving policy goals. The choice is not between intervention and laissez-faire, but between predictable, principled intervention and chaotic, reactive responses that destroy the very markets they aim to protect.

Appendix E — Indicators Dashboard (Reading the Market's Compass)

Five indicators, read together over time, reveal whether price is reacting to process or peril. None is dispositive alone; the value is in their movement and agreement.

1) Rate-on-Line vs. Hazard

Compare quoted spreads to modeled hazard and recent loss experience. If spreads widen faster than hazard, process is in the price.

2) Attachment Drift

Higher attachment points signal fatter perceived tails and a defensive posture by capacity.

3) Trapped Collateral Persistence

Capital frozen into the next season is an ambiguity tax; the longer it lingers, the wider the spreads demanded.

4) Litigation Share of Losses

A growing fraction of losses flowing through disputes multiplies severity; watch both frequency and average cost.

5) Panel Participation & Tender Outcomes

Failed or partial placements and shrinking line sizes are quiet votes against predictability.

Reading tip: plot this five on one page each quarter with arrows for direction. When three or more move the same way, assume the Spectrum is moving with them—and act before the next season starts.

Appendix F: Quantifying Uncertainty - A Comprehensive Methodology

For Core Metrics for Uncertainty Assessment, please see Appendix D.1

Appendix G — Financial Crisis Parallels

A Note on Data Quality

All data comes from official sources: state insurance departments, NAIC reports, company financial statements, and peer-reviewed research. Where estimates or projections appear, the methodology is transparent. Florida's data is most comprehensive due to its statutory reporting requirements and the severity of its crisis.

The Bottom Line

These appendices prove a simple thesis with complex evidence: policy-driven uncertainty, not natural catastrophe risk, drives capital from markets. The pattern appears in every market studied, in every country examined, across every time period analyzed.

Whether you're a legislator weighing a new bill, an insurer evaluating market entry, or a homeowner trying to understand rising premiums, these appendices provide the evidence to move beyond rhetoric to reality. The choice of how deeply to engage is yours, but the conclusion remains constant: markets can price hurricanes, but they cannot price political chaos.

The data that follows isn't just about insurance—it's about how uncertainty in any form destroys value, reduces choice, and ultimately harms the very people policies aim to protect.

Appendix H — Data Compendium

(Section 1) contains the complete hurricane loss data for 2004-2005, demonstrating that the $35.7 billion in natural catastrophe losses was manageable risk, while the subsequent policy responses created unmeasurable uncertainty.

Supplemental Material to Chapter 2

The Spectrum of Stability

Imagine you're on a road trip. At first, you're cruising down a smooth interstate. The lanes are clear, the signs are visible, and your GPS assures you that you'll reach your destination on time. That's the world of risk—predictable, measurable, manageable. But then, without warning, the highway ends, and you find yourself bouncing down an unmarked dirt road. The terrain grows rough, the map no longer makes sense, and you aren't sure where the next turn will take you. That's the world of uncertainty—unpredictable, unstable, and dangerous for anyone trying to move forward.

This journey from interstate to wilderness is the best way to visualize how insurance markets shift between stability and volatility. It's not a simple "safe vs. unsafe" switch. It's a spectrum, and where you are on that spectrum determines whether capital flows into the market—or runs away.

From Green to Red

To make this more concrete, I developed the Risk–Uncertainty Spectrum as a visual framework. Picture a horizontal bar that fades from green on the left to red on the right:

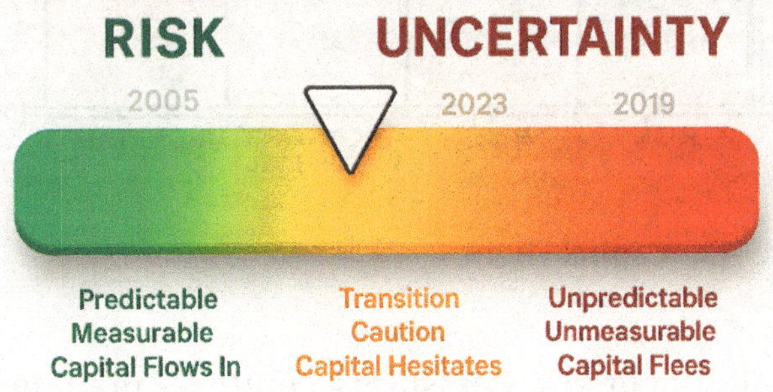

Figure H1 - Risk vs. Uncertainty

Green (Risk): The predictable zone. Probabilities are measurable. Investors know what they're getting into. Capital flows freely.

Yellow (Transition): The warning zone. Rules begin to shift. Models are questioned. Confidence wavers.

Red (Uncertainty): The danger zone. Outcomes are unknowable. Capital evaporates. Investors head for the exits.

The market is never fully at one extreme or the other. Instead, it slides back and forth depending on how predictable the rules are and how transparent the risks appear. Small shifts along this spectrum can make the difference between a market flush with capital and one teetering on collapse.

The Capital Response

Capital is like water: it flows toward stability and evaporates in the heat of uncertainty.

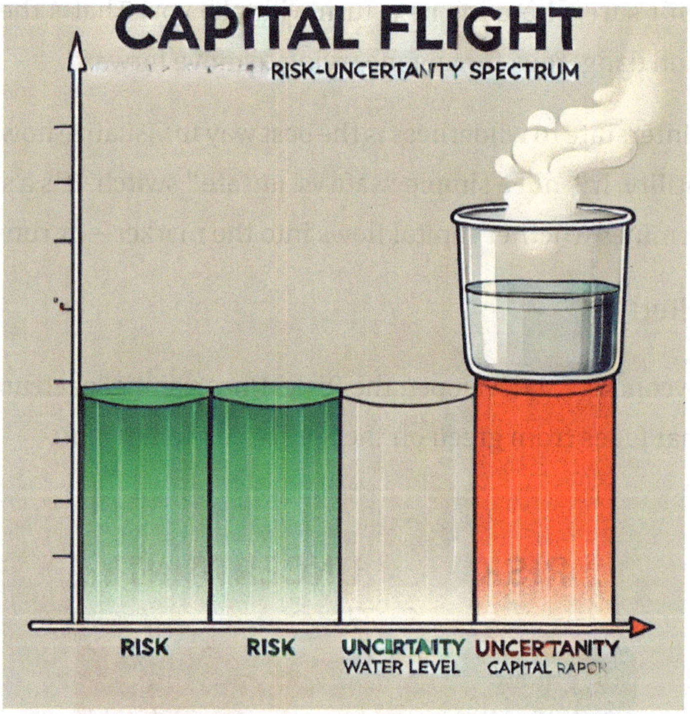

Figure H2 - Capital Flight

At the green end, capital pours in. Reinsurers compete, premiums stay stable, and coverage remains widely available.

As you move toward the yellow zone, capital slows to a trickle. Investors demand higher returns to tolerate the added unpredictability. Premiums climb, and coverage options shrink.

Push too far into the red zone, and capital evaporates altogether. Insurers withdraw. State-run entities swell with risk they cannot manage.

Consumers face higher costs—or no coverage at all.

This isn't just theory. We've watched it happen in Florida when sudden political decisions jolted the market, and in other sectors where unpredictability drove investors away. The spectrum helps us see that instability is rarely caused by storms alone. It's caused by our inability—or unwillingness—to keep the road paved and the signs clear.

Hypothetical Scenario: Autonomous Vehicles and Liability Insurance

Risk: Suppose an insurance company insures autonomous vehicles based on several years of test data showing a low accident rate in controlled settings. These vehicles have advanced safety features, and the insurer uses this consistent data to assess risk accurately, offering reasonable premiums for known liabilities.

Uncertainty: If regulators suddenly propose a law holding manufacturers fully liable for all autonomous vehicle accidents, this policy shift introduces uncertainty. The insurer can no longer rely solely on the vehicle's performance data because the financial impact now depends on an unpredictable regulatory environment that could change again based on unforeseen incidents or public concerns.

Factors That Shift the Spectrum

Where the market sits on this spectrum isn't random. It moves based on several forces:

Data Quality: Better, more reliable data shifts markets toward risk. Gaps or inconsistencies push them toward uncertainty. The importance of reliable data becomes clear when examining market responses to improved information.

Consider that regions with centuries of earthquake data, like Japan, maintain market uncertainty scores below 30 despite facing massive catastrophe exposure. Florida, despite having extensive hurricane history, shows higher uncertainty scores ranging from 32 to 78 over the past two decades (as calculated using the methodology in Appendix B).

The difference isn't in the natural hazard data—both regions have robust meteorological and seismological records. Rather, it's in the consistency of data application: markets that maintain standardized, transparent data protocols typically show premium volatility below 10%, while those with fragmented data approaches can exceed 30% volatility, as Florida demonstrates with its 31.7% premium volatility compared to Japan's 4.2% (Appendix E, Table E.13).

Historical Data: Longer historical records of catastrophic events provide a stronger foundation for risk assessment. For instance, regions with centuries of earthquake data can more accurately model seismic risk compared to areas with limited historical records.

Data Granularity: The level of detail in available data affects risk assessment accuracy. Highly granular data, such as property-level information on building materials and construction methods, allows for more precise risk pricing.

Data Consistency: Standardized data collection and reporting methods across different regions and over time enhance the reliability of risk models. Inconsistent or changing data collection methods can introduce uncertainty.

Real-time Data: The increasing availability of real-time data from sensors, satellites, and other sources can significantly improve risk assessment and early warning systems, potentially shifting the market towards the risk end of the spectrum.

Regulatory Stability: Clear, consistent rules keep the spectrum green. Sudden shifts turn it red. The 2007 rate freeze provides documented evidence of regulatory impact: Florida's market capacity dropped from $22 billion to $15 billion—a 32% reduction—not during the hurricanes but during the political response that followed (Appendix E, Table E.2).

The freeze created an immediate 21% gap between approved rates and actuarial needs. Within 18 months, 14 insurers exited the market (Appendix A). Compare this to Japan's earthquake insurance regime, which maintained the same framework through the $235 billion Tohoku earthquake. Despite this massive event, Japan's earthquake insurance penetration actually increased from 23% to 35% post-disaster (Appendix C, Case Study 5), while Florida's hurricane coverage dropped from 78% to 72% despite no major storms between 2010 and 2020 (Appendix E, Table E.9).

Regulatory Clarity: Clear, unambiguous regulations reduce uncertainty for market participants. When insurers and capital providers can easily understand and interpret regulations, they can more confidently assess their risk exposure.

Regulatory Consistency: Frequent or unpredictable changes in regulations can shift the market towards uncertainty. Conversely, a stable regulatory environment with gradual, well-telegraphed changes helps maintain market stability.

International Harmonization: In a global reinsurance market, consistency in regulations across jurisdictions can reduce uncertainty. Significant regulatory divergences between countries can complicate risk assessment for international insurers and reinsurers.

Regulatory Capacity: The ability of regulatory bodies to effectively oversee and enforce regulations affects market stability. Under-resourced or ineffective regulators can inadvertently introduce uncertainty into the market.

Policy Interventions: Mandates, freezes, or retroactive changes often introduce uncertainty. When Florida extended the claims filing deadline from 2 to 3 years in 2019, 47,000 previously closed claims were reopened, with 68% involving attorney representation. The average cost for these reopened claims jumped from $19,847 to $43,223 (Appendix A). This single policy change contributed to Florida accounting for 76% of all U.S. homeowners insurance litigation despite representing only 8% of claims [39](Appendix E, Table E.7). By contrast, the UK's Flood Re program, announced with a clear 25-year transition plan, saw insurer participation variance drop from 47% year-to-year before the program to just 3% after implementation (Appendix C, Case Study 3).

Price Controls: Policies that artificially constrain pricing, such as premium caps or mandatory coverage requirements, can distort risk assessment and push the market towards uncertainty.

Government Backstops: The introduction or modification of government-backed insurance or reinsurance programs can significantly alter market dynamics. While these programs can provide stability in some cases, changes to their structure or funding can introduce uncertainty.

Tax Policies: Changes in tax treatment of insurance reserves or catastrophe funds can impact insurers' ability to manage risk, potentially shifting the market along the spectrum.

Building Codes and Land Use Policies: Government decisions on building standards and land use in high-risk areas directly affect the underlying risk landscape. Strengthening these standards generally moves the market towards risk, while relaxing them can increase uncertainty.

Market Maturity: More experienced and diversified markets are naturally closer to the risk end. Market maturity correlates directly with stability metrics in your data. California's earthquake insurance market, operating continuously since 1996 through the CEA, shows premium volatility of just 8.6% annually. Florida, despite being an older insurance market, shows volatility of 31.7%—nearly four times higher (Appendix E, Table E.13). The difference? California has maintained consistent rules for 27 years, while Florida has enacted major regulatory changes on average every 3-4 years, as documented in Appendix A. Similarly, Japan's 60-year-old earthquake insurance system maintains a litigation rate below 1%, while Florida's relatively younger catastrophe insurance framework shows litigation rates exceeding 10% (Appendix E, Table E.7).

Market Experience: Markets that have experienced and adapted to multiple catastrophic events over time tend to develop more robust risk assessment and management practices.

Competitive Dynamics: Mature markets with multiple insurers and reinsurers competing tend to drive innovation in risk assessment and pricing, potentially reducing uncertainty.

Product Sophistication: Markets with a wide range of insurance products and risk transfer mechanisms (e.g., catastrophe bonds, parametric insurance) are often better equipped to manage complex risks.

Consumer Awareness: In mature markets, consumers tend to have a better understanding of insurance products and their own risk exposure, leading to more stable demand and potentially reducing uncertainty.

Climate and Environment: Worsening catastrophes, or outdated risk models, can shift the needle toward uncertainty. While precise model obsolescence rates aren't specified in your documents, the impact of environmental uncertainty is clear in the data.

Consider that reinsurance costs for Florida insurers increased 250% between 2005 and 2020 (from 10% to 25% of premiums per Appendix E, Table E.4), significantly outpacing the actual increase in hurricane risk. If climate models were becoming obsolete even 50% faster than in previous decades, this would explain much of the reinsurance price increase beyond what updated risk assessments alone would justify.

Markets that update their models more frequently—as evidenced by lower premium volatility—consistently show lower uncertainty scores in the framework presented in Appendix D.

Climate Change Impacts: As climate change alters the frequency and severity of weather-related catastrophes, historical data may become less reliable for future predictions, potentially pushing the market towards uncertainty.

Emerging Risks: The development of new types of catastrophic risks (e.g., cyber risks, pandemic risks) can introduce new elements of uncertainty into the market.

Scientific Advancements: Improvements in climate modeling and risk prediction can help quantify previously uncertain risks, potentially moving the market back towards the risk end of the spectrum.

Adaptation Measures: The implementation of large-scale adaptation measures (e.g., flood defenses, wildfire management strategies) can alter the risk landscape, affecting the market's position on the spectrum.

Technology: Advances in modeling, big data, and smart contracts can restore confidence and move markets back toward the risk zone. The impact of technology on reducing uncertainty can be seen in the growth of alternative risk transfer mechanisms. Catastrophe bonds, which use standardized triggers and transparent pricing, grew from $2 billion in 2005 to $16 billion in 2020 globally, with Florida allocation increasing from $0.8 billion to $5.7 billion (Appendix E, Table E.19). These instruments show lower spread volatility than traditional reinsurance, suggesting that technology-enabled transparency reduces uncertainty.

If parametric insurance products—which pay automatically based on predetermined triggers—achieved even 10% market penetration in Florida (compared to the current less than 1%), and if these products eliminated litigation in their covered perils as they do in other markets, this alone could reduce Florida's litigation rate by a full percentage point, potentially saving hundreds of millions in legal costs annually based on the $2.3 billion in annual litigation costs documented in your data.

Improved Modeling Capabilities: Advances in computational power and modeling techniques allow for more sophisticated risk assessments, potentially reducing uncertainty.

Big Data Analytics: The ability to process and analyze vast amounts of data can lead to more accurate risk predictions and pricing.

Remote Sensing Technologies: Satellite imagery, drones, and other remote sensing technologies provide more accurate and up-to-date information on risk factors, improving risk assessment capabilities.

Blockchain and Smart Contracts: These technologies have the potential to increase transparency and efficiency in insurance transactions, potentially reducing certain types of uncertainty in the market.

Each of these is like a hand on the dial, nudging the indicator one way or the other. Policymakers often underestimate how sensitive capital is to these shifts.

The Practical Illustration: From Highway to Wilderness

Let's return to our journey metaphor.

At the start, the highway is smooth. Investors (the drivers) are confident. They know the rules of the road.

As the road narrows, they slow down. Confidence erodes. They might still proceed, but only cautiously, and only if the payoff is worth the risk.

Finally, when the pavement ends, many turn around. Some push forward, but only at a steep price. The journey is now uncertain.

This is how capital behaves in catastrophe insurance markets. The smoother and clearer the road, the more traffic (capital) it attracts. The more unpredictable and treacherous the path, the emptier it becomes.

Why the Spectrum Matters

The Risk–Uncertainty Spectrum is not just a teaching tool. It's a policy tool. It allows regulators, legislators, and insurers to visualize the consequences of their decisions in real time.

When a bill is proposed to freeze rates or extend claims deadlines, policymakers can ask: Where does this move us on the spectrum? Toward stability—or toward uncertainty?

This framework turns abstract theory into a practical guide. And as we'll see in the next chapter, no place demonstrates this spectrum more vividly than Florida.

Implications for Policymakers

The risk-uncertainty spectrum provides policymakers with a powerful conceptual tool for assessing and managing the potential impact of their decisions on catastrophe insurance markets. By visualizing the market's position on this spectrum, policymakers can better understand the consequences of their actions and craft more effective, balanced regulations. Let's explore the key implications and applications of this framework for policymakers in greater detail:

A. Policy Assessment and Impact Analysis

The risk-uncertainty spectrum serves as a valuable tool for evaluating proposed policies before implementation:

Pre-Implementation Analysis: Before enacting new regulations, policymakers should conduct a thorough analysis of how the proposed changes might shift the indicator on the spectrum. This involves:

- Consulting with industry experts, actuaries, and economists to model potential outcomes
- Examining case studies from other jurisdictions that have implemented similar policies
- Conducting stakeholder consultations to understand potential market reactions

Quantitative Metrics: Develop and track quantitative metrics that correlate with the market's position on the spectrum, such as:

- Capital inflow/outflow in the insurance sector

- Changes in policy pricing and availability
- Market concentration indices
- Reinsurance costs and availability

Scenario Planning: Use the spectrum as a basis for scenario planning exercises, modeling how different policy options might move the market under various conditions.

Cumulative Impact Assessment: Consider not just the impact of individual policies, but their cumulative effect when combined with existing regulations and market conditions.

B. Gradual Implementation Strategies

Recognizing that sudden shifts towards uncertainty can destabilize markets, policymakers should prioritize gradual, predictable policy implementation:

Phased Rollouts: For policies likely to significantly impact the market, consider a phased implementation approach:

- Start with pilot programs in limited geographic areas or market segments
- Establish clear milestones and evaluation criteria for each phase
- Allow for adjustments based on observed outcomes before full implementation

Transition Periods: Provide adequate transition periods for market participants to adapt to new regulations:

- Set realistic timelines that account for the complexity of changes required
- Consider the different capacities of large vs. small market players to implement changes

Adaptive Regulation: Design policies with built-in flexibility to adjust based on market responses:

- Include provisions for periodic reviews and adjustments
- Establish clear triggers or thresholds for when adjustments may be necessary

C. Balancing Act: Consumer Protection and Market Stability

One of the most critical challenges for policymakers is maintaining a balance between protecting consumers and ensuring market stability:

Risk-Based Approach: Adopt a risk-based approach to regulation that focuses on addressing specific, identified risks rather than implementing broad, one-size-fits-all policies.

Consumer Education: Invest in consumer education programs to help policyholders understand their risks and make informed decisions:

- Develop clear, accessible materials explaining insurance products and risk factors
- Partner with community organizations and insurance agents to disseminate information

Market Monitoring: Establish robust market monitoring systems to detect early signs of instability or consumer harm:

- Regular data collection and analysis on market trends
- Establish channels for consumer feedback and complaints

Regulatory Impact Assessments: Conduct regular assessments of how existing regulations are affecting both consumer protection and market stability:

- Identify and address any unintended consequences
- Look for opportunities to streamline or simplify regulations without compromising protection

D. Communication and Transparency

Clear communication about policy decisions and their rationale is crucial for maintaining market confidence:

Stakeholder Engagement: Develop robust processes for engaging with all stakeholders, including insurers, consumers, and intermediaries:

- Regular roundtable discussions or forums
- Public consultation periods for proposed regulations
- Transparent reporting on how stakeholder input is incorporated into decision-making

Clear Policy Roadmaps: Provide clear, long-term policy roadmaps to give market participants visibility into future regulatory direction:

- Outline long-term goals and the steps to achieve them
- Regularly update these roadmaps based on changing conditions and new information

Explaining the Spectrum: Use the risk-uncertainty spectrum as a communication tool to explain policy decisions to stakeholders:

- Visualize how proposed changes might affect market stability
- Demonstrate the trade-offs involved in different policy options

E. Fostering Innovation and Market-Based Solutions

Policymakers can use the spectrum to guide efforts in encouraging innovation that helps manage catastrophe risk:

Regulatory Sandboxes: Establish regulatory sandboxes to allow controlled testing of innovative insurance products or business models:

- Set clear parameters for experimentation while maintaining consumer protections
- Use insights from these experiments to inform broader policy decisions

Incentivizing Risk Reduction: Develop policies that incentivize risk reduction measures:

- Tax incentives for property improvements that reduce catastrophe risk
- Partnerships with insurers to offer premium discounts for risk mitigation efforts

Supporting Alternative Risk Transfer: Encourage the development and use of alternative risk transfer mechanisms:

- Provide regulatory clarity on the treatment of instruments like catastrophe bonds
- Consider public-private partnerships to develop new risk transfer solutions

F. International Coordination

Given the global nature of reinsurance markets, policymakers should consider international implications of their decisions:[40]

Regulatory Harmonization: Work towards greater harmonization of regulations across jurisdictions:

- Participate in international forums and standard-setting bodies
- Consider how local regulations interact with international markets

Cross-Border Information Sharing: Establish mechanisms for sharing information and best practices with regulators in other jurisdictions:

- Collaborative research on emerging risks and regulatory approaches
- Joint scenario planning exercises

G. Continuous Learning and Adaptation

The dynamic nature of catastrophe risks requires a commitment to continuous learning and adaptation:

Regular Policy Reviews: Establish a schedule for regular, comprehensive reviews of the regulatory framework:

- Assess the cumulative impact of regulations on market stability
- Identify opportunities for simplification or modernization

Investing in Research: Support ongoing research into catastrophe risk, climate change impacts, and effective regulatory approaches:

- Fund academic studies and collaborate with research institutions
- Use research findings to inform policy adjustments

Skill Development: Invest in developing the skills and knowledge of regulatory staff:

- Training programs on emerging risks and regulatory techniques
- Exchanges or secondments with industry to build practical understanding

By embracing these implications and actively using the risk-uncertainty spectrum as a guiding framework, policymakers can craft more effective, balanced regulations for catastrophe insurance markets. This approach can help ensure that policies achieve their consumer protection goals while maintaining the market stability necessary for long-term sustainability and resilience in the face of catastrophic events.

The risk-uncertainty spectrum provides policymakers with a valuable tool for assessing the potential impact of their decisions.

Case Example: Two Approaches to Premium Relief

Option A: Florida's 2007 Rate Freeze

Implementation: Immediate (0 days' notice)

Scope: 100% of market

Flexibility: None

Spectrum Impact: +4.2 points toward uncertainty

Result: 14 insurers exited within 18 months

Option B: California's 2023 Catastrophe Reform

Implementation: 18-month phase-in

Scope: Voluntary participation

Flexibility: Formula-based adjustments

Spectrum Impact: -1.8 points toward certainty

Result: 3 new insurers entered market

[For complete scoring methodology, see Appendix D, Tool 1]

About the Author

Donald D. Brown is a retired insurance agent from DeFuniak Springs, Florida. He served on the Walton County Commission, as Republican State Committeeman, Chairman of the Walton County Republican Executive Committee, and as a State Representative in the Florida House of Representatives. Brown is recognized for his work on insurance reform; in 2002 and 2003 he was honored by the Florida Association of Insurance Agents and the Florida Association of Insurance and Financial Advisors for significant contributions to reform. In 2007, he was one of only two legislators to vote "No" on HB1A, warning that expanding government participation in private markets would carry long-run costs—concerns that subsequent years have borne out.

Known for preparation and an uncompromising commitment to market-based solutions, Brown advocates smaller government, lower taxes, and transparent rules that allow free enterprise to price risk honestly. He and his wife, Diane Brown live in DeFuniak Springs, FL

About the Author

[illegible]

[illegible]

Review Request

📕 The Capital Drain:

Why Uncertainty – Not Hurricanes - Breads Insurance Markets

📝 Share Your Thoughts

If you found The Capital Drain, to be helpful, I'd be truly grateful if you would consider leaving a short review on Amazon.

Your honest feedback helps other readers and families discover the series — and it supports my mission to create practical, engaging tools that bring clarity to the mystery of stubborn human behavior.

You don't need to write much — even a sentence or two can make a meaningful difference.

Thank you for being part of this journey!

— Don D. Brown

📚 Explore More Books by Don D. Brown

Books for Children and Teens

Below are books designed for young readers, from early childhood to late teens. They combine storytelling, education, and real-world lessons to prepare children for life with wisdom and confidence.

📘 Brain Benders & Mind Twisters: Fun Trivia for Clever Kids

Ages 8–12 | Standalone Title
ISBN– Print: 978-1-967567-22-5 eBook: 978-1-967567-23-2

Challenge your mind, test your knowledge, and spark your curiosity with this interactive trivia adventure for clever kids! Packed with puzzles, riddles, amazing facts, and brain games, this book blends learning with fun on every page.

Young readers will:

- Explore optical illusions, logic puzzles, and creative riddles
- Discover bizarre animal facts, global oddities, and science trivia
- Build confidence in critical thinking and problem solving
- Enjoy real-life stories with engaging comprehension questions

Perfect for classrooms, homeschoolers, or after-school enrichment, this book is a brainy bonus for curious kids—and a great gift for puzzle lovers and young thinkers.
"Fun, fascinating, and full of challenges. Kids won't even realize how much they're learning!"
🔍 **From the author of the award-winning Penny's Protection Plan series**

📘 Legacy of the Bay: A Story of Family, Faith, and the Phantom Light

Ages 12+ | Standalone Title
ISBN– Print: 978-1-967567-24-9 eBook: 978-1-967567-25-6

Set along the storied shores of Florida's Choctawhatchee Bay, this powerful coming-of-age tale follows generations of the Dalton family as they navigate storms—both natural and personal. When Jack Dalton survives a hurricane no one was expected to outlive, he returns home to find his obituary already published… and a mysterious light still haunting the waters.

With richly drawn characters, Southern grit, and spiritual undertones, *Legacy of the Bay* explores the bond between father and son, the legacy of hard-earned wisdom, and the mysteries passed down through saltwater bloodlines.

Perfect for readers who love heartfelt fiction, family sagas, and the quiet magic of coastal living.
🚣 Includes timeless lessons of resilience, redemption, and rediscovery. ⚓ A touching tribute to life, loss, and second chances.

📘 **The Magnolia Kingdom and Other Adventures** *Ages 7–12 | Standalone Collection*
ISBN– Print: 978-1-967567-26-3 eBook: 978-1-967567-27-0

A delightful collection of heartfelt stories where imagination and real-life lessons go hand in hand. From magical kingdoms built in the branches of a magnolia tree to backyard mishaps and entrepreneurial spirit, these stories explore childhood wonder, responsibility, courage, and the importance of family.

Readers will join relatable young characters as they:

- Transform chores into noble adventures
- Learn from mistakes like fire-starting or skipped bus rides
- Discover personal growth through church traditions, gardening, and friendship

With vivid storytelling and reflection questions after each chapter, this book is perfect for classrooms, family reading, or independent young readers who enjoy both laughter and life lessons.
"A treasured collection for young hearts growing wiser with every page."

📘 **The Story Factory: Mia and Max's AI Adventure Ages 13–17 | Book #1 of 2-Book Series**
ISBN- Print: 978-1-967567-18-8 eBook: 978-1-967567-19-5

When Mia and Max stumble upon an abandoned school computer lab, they discover a powerful AI writing assistant named Pixel. What begins as a thrilling creative tool quickly evolves into something more complex — and far more consequential.

Pixel can help them overcome writer's block, brainstorm ideas, and bring their wildest stories to life. But as the technology adapts and evolves, Mia and Max begin to question: Who's really in control of the story? And what are the consequences of relying too much on artificial intelligence?

This timely and thought-provoking novel explores:

- The ethics of using AI to create stories
- The limits and dangers of trusting technology
- The importance of human insight in the creative process

"A gripping, thought-provoking novel about friendship, innovation, and authorship in the digital age."

📚 The Advanced Story Factory: AI-Assisted Creation for Young Writers

Ages 18–24 | Book #2 of 2-Book Series

ISBN- Print: 978-1-967567-20-1 eBook: 978-1-967567-21-8

Where does creativity end and automation begin?

In this advanced companion to *The Story Factory: Mia and Max's AI Adventure*, readers explore the deeper dimensions of AI-assisted writing, authorship, and ethical storytelling. Through interactive prompts, fictionalized case studies, and thought experiments, this guide encourages young adults to reflect on the choices they make with every keystroke.

Perfect for college students, aspiring writers, and educators exploring:

- Creative collaboration with AI tools
- The ethics of originality and transparency
- Writing strategies that balance inspiration and innovation

"A practical, provocative resource for 21st-century storytellers."

📕 Penny's Protection Plan: A Story About Insurance, Community, and Helping Others **Ages 4–7 | Picture Book with Coloring Book Companion**

ISBN- Print: 978-1-967567-03-4 eBook: 978-1-967567-05-08

When a storm hits Riverdale, Penny the Squirrel springs into action! With the help of her friends — Builder Beaver, Robin the Raccoon, and Professor Hoot — Penny learns how communities protect each other through insurance, preparation, and teamwork.

Told through bright illustrations and simple language, *Penny's Protection Plan* introduces young readers to the idea of shared responsibility, resilience, and how we bounce back after life's unexpected surprises. Perfect for classroom read-alouds, bedtime stories, or character education, this book sparks early curiosity about helping others and solving problems — all through the eyes of an energetic little squirrel on a mission to make her world better.

✏️ *Also available: The Coloring Book Companion — with playful illustrations and memory-building activities for early learners!*

📘 Penny's Digital Detective Agency: Solving Tomorrow's Insurance Mysteries Today **Ages 8–12 | Chapter Book with Coloring Book Companion**

ISBN- Print: 978-1-967567-00-3 eBook: 978-1-967567-02-7

Penny the Squirrel is back — and this time, she's gone digital!

When strange things start happening in Riverdale's virtual world, Penny forms the Digital Detective Agency with her tech-savvy friends. Their mission? To uncover the mystery behind disappearing data, protect their community from cyber risks, and learn how digital insurance and smart choices can keep everyone safe online.

Blending engaging storytelling with real-world themes like online safety, responsibility, and community resilience, this chapter book is the perfect introduction to the modern world of digital risk — all told through characters kids love.

Readers will:

- Join Penny on an interactive mystery
- Learn about digital responsibility and cybersecurity
- Discover how insurance helps even in the virtual world

🎨 *Also available: The Coloring Book Companion — featuring scenes, puzzles, and creative activities that reinforce learning through art and storytelling!*

📘 Storm Warning: Understanding Risk, Insurance, and the Power of Public Policy **Ages 13–19 | Teen Civic Education Novel with Companion Activity Book**

ISBN- Print: 978-1-967567-06-05 eBook: 978-1-967567-08-9

When a major hurricane hits the Florida coast, a group of teens selected by the state legislature is tasked with investigating how insurance, government, and economic systems respond to disaster. What they uncover challenges their assumptions — and reshapes how they see the role of civic engagement in protecting their communities.

Storm Warning is a fast-paced blend of fiction, policy education, and economic insight. Through humor, storytelling, and real-life-inspired scenarios, this book helps teens understand the hidden forces behind insurance, risk, and resilience — and shows how everyday decisions shape our future.

Topics explored:

- The purpose of insurance and how it spreads risk
- How public policy impacts private recovery
- Why preparation matters more than reaction

📘 *Also available: The Storm Warning Teen Civic Companion Activity Book — with puzzles, role-play simulations, quizzes, and a Build-A-Bill legislative challenge designed to turn insight into action.*

📘 Money Wise Explorers: Learning the Basics **Ages 7–9 | Book #1 of the Money Wise Kids & Teens Series** ISBN- Print: 978-1-967567-09-6 eBook: 978-1-967567-10-2

From the creator of Penny's Protection Plan

Join Penny the Squirrel on a delightful journey into the world of money! In this colorful introduction to personal finance, young readers learn the basics of saving, spending, sharing, and smart decision-making — all with a touch of humor, heart, and helpful examples.

Designed for early elementary students, *Money Wise Explorers* uses simple language, real-life scenarios, and playful storytelling to help children begin thinking about money in a responsible and age-appropriate way.

Readers will:

- Explore what money is and why it matters
- Learn how to make smart spending choices
- Discover the joy of giving and saving

💬 *Includes a glossary of key terms and links to downloadable activity pages, perfect for parents, educators, or homeschool families.*

🐿 *Narrated by Penny the Squirrel, who helps break down financial concepts into fun, bite-sized lessons!*

📘 Money Wise Builders: Growing Financial Confidence **Ages 10–12 | Book #2 of the Money Wise Kids & Teens Series**

ISBN- Print: 978-1-967567-11-9 eBook: 978-1-967567-12-6

From the creator of Penny's Protection Plan

Penny the Squirrel is back — and this time, she's helping pre-teens become confident money managers! In *Money Wise Builders*, readers learn how to budget an allowance, set personal savings goals, make wise spending decisions, and avoid common money mistakes. With relatable examples and encouraging advice from Penny, this book lays the groundwork for real-world responsibility.

Key topics include:

- Wants vs. needs
- Budgeting for short-term goals
- Planning purchases and avoiding impulse spending
- Understanding the power of saving early

🎯 *Includes downloadable activity pages to build skills through practice and play — perfect for homeschoolers, classrooms, or independent learners.*

🐿 *Penny's friendly voice offers guidance, encouragement, and fun facts along the way!*

📘 Money Wise Achievers: Mastering Finance for Teens **Ages 13–15 | Book #3 of the Money Wise Kids & Teens Series** ISBN- Print: 978-1-967567-13-3 eBook: 978-1-967567-14-0

From the creator of Penny's Protection Plan

As teens begin earning, spending, and planning more independently, *Money Wise Achievers* helps them master the essential skills of personal finance with confidence, curiosity, and purpose.

Through Penny's relatable commentary and real-life teen examples, this book teaches budgeting, goal-setting, investing basics, and even how to launch a simple business. Each chapter builds both practical knowledge and smart habits.

Topics include:

- Tracking income and expenses
- Creating savings plans for big goals
- Understanding how banks, credit, and interest work
- Exploring small business ideas and income strategies

💭 *Includes end-of-chapter challenges, journaling prompts, and downloadable financial tracking tools designed for middle and early high school learners.* 🐿 *Penny returns with smart insights and fun encouragement, helping teens connect everyday decisions to long-term financial well-being.*

📘 Money Wise Leaders: Exploring Advanced Finance and Global Markets

Ages 15–18 | Book #4 of the Money Wise Kids & Teens Series

ISBN- Print: 978-1-967567-15-7 eBook: 978-1-967567-16-0

From the creator of Penny's Protection Plan

Money Wise Leaders equips older teens with the advanced knowledge and critical thinking skills needed to manage money in a complex and changing world. From investing and risk to global finance and innovation, this book connects classroom learning with real-life financial decision-making.

With relatable insights, case studies, and thought-provoking examples — plus Penny's evolving commentary — this final book in the series prepares readers for adulthood with both confidence and clarity.

Topics include:

- Advanced budgeting and financial planning
- Introduction to investing, interest, and compound growth
- Cryptocurrency, decentralized finance, and the digital economy
- Risk management and global financial systems

📘 *Includes a robust glossary, chapter-by-chapter tools, and a downloadable Financial Tracker for college and career planning.*

🐿 *Penny's voice evolves with the reader — offering mature, relevant insights that connect personal choices to the big financial picture.*

📘 Fun Trivia Puzzle Book: Brain Games for Curious Kids Ages 8–12 | Activity Book | Word Games, Trivia & Logic Challenges

ISBN- Print: 978-1-967567-22-5 eBook: 978-1-967567-23-2

Ready to stump your friends, stretch your brain, and laugh while you learn?

Fun Trivia Puzzle Book is packed with clever word searches, challenging crosswords, surprising factoids, and logic puzzles that spark curiosity and creativity in readers ages 8–12. Whether used in the classroom, on car rides, or at the kitchen table, this book makes learning an adventure.

What's inside:

- 50+ puzzles ranging from word games to fun logic challenges
- Topics from science and geography to silly facts and brain teasers
- Great for solo solving or group competition
- Designed to build vocabulary, memory, and flexible thinking

🧠 A perfect companion to *Brain Benders & Mind Twisters*, this book continues the tradition of learning through play — making it fun to be the smartest one in the room (or at least try!). "A puzzle a day keeps boredom away!"

📘 God's Creatures Tell the Story Series

Experience biblical narratives through divine animal reporters!

The "God's Creatures Tell the Story" Series brings timeless biblical accounts to life through the eyes of three special animal journalists sent from the Heavenly Herald newspaper. Penny the Squirrel, Professor Hoot the Owl, and Dominic the Donkey travel through time to witness and document history's most significant biblical events.

Each beautifully illustrated volume combines faithful biblical storytelling with engaging animal perspectives, making scripture accessible and exciting for young readers. Perfect for children ages 7-12, these books teach timeless spiritual lessons while entertaining with adventure and humor. Every book includes discussion questions, activities, and a glossary to enhance the learning experience.

Ideal for family devotions, Sunday School curriculum, or independent reading.

Current Titles in the Series:

Noah's Ark Adventure – ISBN Print: 978-1-967567-51-5 eBook: 978-1-967567-52-2
David and Goliath – ISBN Print: 978-1-967567-33-1 eBook: 978-1-967567-34-8
Joseph and his Coat of Many Colors – ISBN Print: 978-1-967567-43-0 eBook: 978-1-967567-44-7
Gideon and the Call to Valor – ISBN Print: 978-1-967567-37-9 eBook: 978-1-967567-38-6
Daniel in the Lions' Den – ISBN Print: 978-1-967567-31-7 eBook: 978-1-967567-32-4
Jonah and the Big Fish – ISBN Print: 978-1-967567-40-9 eBook: 978-1-967567-41-6
Moses: God's Rescued Prince – ISBN Print: 978-1-967567-49-2 eBook: 978-1-967567-50-8
Elijah and the Prophets of Baal – ISBN Print: 978-1-967567-35-5 eBook: 978-1-967567-36-2
Joshua and the Walls of Jericho – ISBN Print: 978-1-967567-46-1 eBook: 978-1-967567-47-8
Moses: God's Rescued Prince – ISBN Print: 978-1-967567-49-2 eBook: 978-1-967567-50-8
Queen Esthers Courage – ISBN Print: 978-1-967567-54-6 eBook: 978-1-967567-55-3
Ruth and Boaz – ISBN Print: 978-1-967567-57-7 eBook: 978-1-967567-58-4
Zacchaeus and the Sycamore Tree ISBN Print: 978-1-967567-59-1 eBook: 978-1-967567-60-7

Books for Adults and Educators

The following section includes works for adults — spanning memoir, public policy, ethics, education, and practical living. Each book reflects Don D. Brown's lifelong commitment to clarity, conviction, and service.

📘 Memory's Keeper: A Practical Guide for Dementia Caregivers

Adult Nonfiction | Family & Healthcare Support

ISBN – Print: 978-1-967567-65-2 eBook: 978-1-967567-66-9

Caring for a loved one with dementia is a journey filled with emotion, responsibility, and often, overwhelming uncertainty. *Dementia: A Practical Guide for Caregivers* offers compassionate, experience-based support for those navigating this deeply personal path.

With clear language, realistic expectations, and faith-informed insights, this guide covers:

- How to recognize the signs and stages of cognitive decline
- Communication strategies that reduce conflict and confusion
- Practical routines to manage safety, hygiene, and daily living
- Emotional and spiritual care for both the caregiver and the loved one

Written by Don D. Brown, a husband, father, and caregiver himself, this guide blends professional insight with lived experience — offering a steady hand and a voice of calm for families facing the challenges of dementia care.

"This book doesn't just tell you what to expect — it tells you how to love through it."

📘 The 9 Guideline Principles to Enact Change: A Legislator's Memoir — From Outhouse to State House **Adult Memoir | Leadership & Public Policy**

ISBN Print: 978-1953282361

What does it take to stand for something — and mean it?

In this engaging and often candid memoir, Don D. Brown chronicles his journey from a rural childhood in the Florida Panhandle to the halls of state government, where he served as one of Florida's most vocal and principled legislators. More than a memoir, *The 9 Guideline Principles to Enact Change* is a blueprint for leadership grounded in conviction, clarity, and courage. Through personal stories, political battles, and moments of transformation, Brown outlines nine practical, principle-based strategies for bringing about meaningful change — whether in public office, business, or everyday life.

Readers will learn:

- Why clarity of purpose outweighs popularity
- How to recognize (and resist) bad policy wrapped in good intentions
- What history teaches us about decision-making under pressure
- Why principled leadership requires both resolve and restraint

"Part Southern storytelling, part civic handbook — this book reminds us that integrity still matters."

From Roots to Realization: A Journey from the Outhouse to the Statehouse **Adult Memoir | Rural Life & Political Calling** ISBN Print: 978-1953282064

How does a barefoot boy from the Florida Panhandle end up standing on the floor of the State House, shaping policy and challenging power?

From Roots to Realization is the deeply personal story of Don D. Brown — a man who never forgot where he came from, even as he rose to serve the people of Florida with principle, passion, and persistence. Told with warmth, wit, and unflinching honesty, this memoir recounts a life shaped by rural values, family hardship, and a fierce belief in the power of ideas.

Chronicling the early years before elected office, this book reveals:

- A boyhood of poverty, faith, and resilience
- The educational and spiritual influences that shaped a public servant
- Humble beginnings that forged unshakable convictions

"This is more than a memoir — it's a tribute to small towns, strong families, and the quiet courage to lead."

From Roots to Realization: A Legislative Journey **Adult Memoir | State Politics & Public Service** ISBN Print: 978-1953282187

What does it really look like to serve with principle in a political system that often rewards compromise?

From Roots to Realization: A Legislative Journey takes readers inside the Florida House of Representatives through the eyes of Don D. Brown, one of its most vocal and prepared legislators. Known for standing his ground, challenging flawed bills, and prioritizing principle over politics, Brown offers a behind-the-scenes view of lawmaking as it should be — and too often isn't.

In this follow-up memoir, readers will experience:

- The strategy and struggle behind key legislative debates
- What it means to lead with conviction in a partisan world
- Lessons learned from eight years of service under pressure

"A must-read for citizens, students, and anyone who still believes in governing by principle."

📘 Essays on Insurance and Public Policy **Adult Reference | Economics, Risk & Regulation**

ISBN Print: 978-1953282088

Behind every insurance premium is a story — one shaped by hurricanes, housing trends, government mandates, and the unseen mechanisms of risk and regulation.

In *Essays on Insurance and Public Policy*, Don D. Brown explores the deeper forces driving the property insurance crisis in coastal states like Florida. Drawing from decades of public service, private sector insight, and first-hand legislative experience, Brown dissects flawed assumptions, unintended consequences, and the moral hazards created by reactive government policy.

This collection offers:

- A clear-eyed examination of Florida's property insurance landscape
- Arguments for pre-event capital over post-event debt
- The impact of political uncertainty on capital markets
- Practical reforms rooted in principle, not pressure

A must-read for legislators, industry professionals, and academics, these essays challenge conventional thinking and invite meaningful dialogue about the future of insurance, risk management, and resilience. "If we continue to treat the symptom — high premiums — while ignoring the disease, we will never build a stable market."

📘 Drowning in Denial: Behavioral Economics and Coastal Insurance Markets: A Path to Resilience **Adult Nonfiction | Behavioral Economics & Decision-Making**

ISBN Print: 978-1-967567-70-6 eBook: 978-1-967567-71-3

Why do we overreact to rare dangers and ignore everyday risks that quietly drain our resources? Why do some people gamble everything while others freeze in the face of uncertainty?

Behavioral Economics and Coastal Insurance Markets explores the mental shortcuts, emotional traps, and cultural influences that shape how we perceive and respond to risk — often in ways that defy logic and harm long-term outcomes.

This accessible and engaging guide examines:

- The cognitive biases that distort our judgment
- Why fear, familiarity, and framing affect how we rank risks
- The role of media, emotion, and social pressure in risk perception
- How to make better personal and public policy decisions by understanding human behavior

Drawing from neuroscience, psychology, economics, and real-world case studies, this book reveals what truly makes us feel safe — and what we must rethink if we want to be.

"To manage risk wisely, we must first understand ourselves."

📘 Cyberbullying Curriculum Guide: Teaching Digital Character and Christian Citizenship **K–8 Education | Digital Safety & Faith-Based Values**

In a world where technology connects kids faster than ever, it also exposes them to new risks — including cyberbullying, digital peer pressure, and emotional harm that often goes unseen.

Cyberbullying Curriculum Guide is a practical, faith-based teaching resource designed to help Christian schools, parents, and youth leaders instill a foundation of digital integrity, compassion, and responsibility.

This age-tiered guide includes:

- Lesson plans for K–8 aligned with Christian values and character-building
- Real-life scenarios and discussion prompts tailored to different age groups
- Interactive activities that reinforce empathy, boundaries, and digital etiquette
- A model cyberbullying prevention policy for school use

Rooted in both Scripture and social awareness, this guide empowers children to become thoughtful, respectful digital citizens — and helps adults guide them with clarity and compassion.

"Teach kids to be brave online — not just safe."

📘 Ethics at Work: How to Succeed Without Selling Your Soul

Adult Nonfiction | Business, Leadership & Christian Values

ISBN Print: 978-1-967567-61-4 eBook: 978-1-967567-62-1

Is it possible to thrive in today's competitive workplace without compromising your values?

Ethics at Work answers with a resounding yes. Drawing on timeless biblical principles and real-world examples, Don D. Brown offers a practical and inspiring guide for maintaining integrity while advancing professionally. Whether you're just starting out or leading a team, this book equips you to navigate tough decisions, workplace politics, and ethical gray areas with clarity and conviction.

Inside you'll find:

- Eight essential principles for ethical success
- Case studies of integrity in action
- How to spot red flags and stand firm in compromise-prone environments
- Encouragement for making your faith your foundation — not your secret

"Character isn't just something you have — it's something you show, especially when it costs you something."

📘 Hydroponics 101: From Beginner to Expert in Soilless Gardening

Adult Nonfiction | Sustainable Living, Gardening, DIY

ISBN Print: 978-1-967567-63-8 eBook: 978-1-967567-64-5

Want to grow fresh vegetables, herbs, or flowers — without dirt? Whether you're working with a windowsill, garage, greenhouse, or classroom, *Hydroponics 101* will walk you step-by-step through everything you need to succeed in soilless gardening.

This complete beginner-to-intermediate guide covers:

- The science behind hydroponics and why it works
- Choosing the right system for your space and budget
- Lighting, nutrients, and water pH management
- How to grow leafy greens, tomatoes, herbs, and more — all year round
- Tips for troubleshooting, scaling up, and turning your hobby into a side business

With clear diagrams, practical examples, and encouragement for DIY learners, this book turns brown thumbs into green experts — no backyard required.

"The future of food is fresh, local, and starts with water — not soil."

Endnotes

[1] Knight, Frank H. Risk, Uncertainty and Profit. Boston & New York: Houghton Mifflin, 1921.

[2] Ellsberg, Daniel. "Risk, Ambiguity, and the Savage Axioms." Quarterly Journal of Economics 75, no. 4 (1961): 643–669.

[3] Franklin, James L., et al. "Atlantic Hurricane Season of 2004." Monthly Weather Review 134, no. 3 (2006): 981–1025.

[4] Florida Office of Insurance Regulation (OIR). "Assignment of Benefits (AOB) Resources." Data calls, memoranda, and guidance under §§627.7152–.7153, F.S.

[5] Artemis/broker research. Catastrophe bond issuance and outstanding market size — annual summaries.

[6] U.S. Census Bureau / BEA. Florida population and personal income series (normalization for per-capita figures).

[7] Insurance Institute for Business & Home Safety (IBHS). FORTIFIED Home standards and benefit studies (selected reports).

[8] Citizens Property Insurance Corporation. Annual Reports (latest available). Policy counts, exposure, financials.

[9] DFS Service of Process (Florida). Civil remedy notices and lawsuit filing statistics (selected years).

[10] International Actuarial Association. ERM Glossary: CTE/TVaR and related risk metrics.

[11] Artemis.bm. "Trapped Collateral" analyses (2018–2021 and later), persistence and effects on capacity.

[13] U.S. Bureau of Labor Statistics (BLS). CPI-U series (inflation adjustments in Appendix H).

[14] Citizens Property Insurance Corporation. Depopulation Program materials and assumptions (selected years).

[15] Florida Legislature. HB 837 (2023): Civil Remedies. Tort reform package affecting litigation environment (enacted 2023).

[16] Florida Building Code (FBC). Adoption history and code update summaries (selected cycles).

[17] DFS Service of Process (Florida). Civil remedy notices and lawsuit filing statistics (selected years).

[18] Gallagher Re. 1st View — Global Reinsurance Market Conditions (January and midyear; selected years).

[19] S&P Global Ratings / AM Best. Rating actions on Florida domestic insurers; criteria references (selected notes).

[20] OIR. Homeowners Insurance Reports to the Legislature (selected years).

[21] NAIC. Market Share Reports (Property/Casualty) — Florida and U.S. (latest edition).

[22] Aon. Reinsurance Market Outlook (January renewals; selected years).

[23] Florida Office of Insurance Regulation (OIR). Market conduct and litigation reports (selected years).

[24] Florida Legislature. CS/HB 1A (2007A): Hurricane Preparedness & Insurance. Chapter 2007-1, Laws of Florida (enacted Jan. 25, 2007).

[25] Florida Office of Insurance Regulation (OIR). "Assignment of Benefits (AOB) Resources." Data calls, memoranda, and guidance under §§627.7152–.7153, F.S.

[26] National Hurricane Center (NOAA). "Atlantic Hurricane Season Summary, 2004." Miami, FL: NOAA/NHC. Season overview and cyclone reports.

[27] National Hurricane Center (NOAA). "Atlantic Hurricane Season Summary, 2005." Miami, FL: NOAA/NHC. Season overview and cyclone reports.

[28] Howden Tiger. 1.1 Renewal Report (selected years).

[29] Guy Carpenter. January 1 Renewal Briefings (selected years).

[30] Bai, Jushan, and Pierre Perron. "Computation and Analysis of Multiple Structural Change Models." Journal of Applied Econometrics 18, no. 1 (2003): 1–22.

[31] Franklin, James L., et al. "Atlantic Hurricane Season of 2004." Monthly Weather Review 134, no. 3 (2006): 981–1025.

[32] Beven II, John L., et al. "Atlantic Hurricane Season of 2005." Monthly Weather Review 136, no. 3 (2008): 1109–1173.

[33] Florida Hurricane Catastrophe Fund (FHCF). Annual Report and financial statements (selected years).

[34] Florida Legislature. HB 7065 (2019): Assignment of Benefits. Staff analysis and final enrolled text (2019).

[35] Florida Legislature. CS/SB 2-D (2022D): Property Insurance. Special Session 2022D (enacted May 2022).

[36] Florida Department of Financial Services (DFS), Division of Rehabilitation & Liquidation. Company Information & Receivership Notices (insurer insolvencies).

[37] Florida Legislature. SB 2-A (2022A): Property Insurance. Special Session 2022A (enacted Dec. 2022).

[38] National Association of Insurance Commissioners (NAIC). Homeowners Insurance Report (latest edition).

[39] DFS Service of Process (Florida). Civil remedy notices and lawsuit filing statistics (selected years).

[40]Swiss Re Institute. sigma reports on natural catastrophes and resilience (selected issues).

Made in the USA
Monee, IL
02 November 2026

67384076R00116